# What is Social Ant

Other *What is . . .?* books available

*Linguistics*
*Psychology*
*Communication Studies*
*Accounting*


*in preparation*

*Engineering*
*Religious Studies*
*Business Studies*

# What is Social Anthropology?

Jean La Fontaine

Emeritus Professor of Social Anthropology,
London School of Economics

Edward Arnold

© Jean La Fontaine 1985

First published in Great Britain 1985 by
Edward Arnold (Publishers) Ltd, 41 Bedford Square, London
WC18 3DQ

Edward Arnold (Australia) Pty Ltd, 80 Waverley Road, Caulfield
East, Victoria 3145, Australia

Edward Arnold, 300 North Charles Street, Baltimore, Maryland
21201, U.S.A.


**British Library Cataloguing in Publication Data**

La Fontaine, Jean
    What is social anthropology?
    1. Ethnology
    I. Title
    306     GN316

    ISBN 0–7131–6445–X

Text set in 10/11pt Times Compugraphic
by Colset Private Ltd., Singapore.
Printed and bound by Richard Clay (The Chaucer Press) Ltd
Bungay, Suffolk.

# Contents

# Preface

This book is a response to the many different people who have, at various times over the years that I have been a social anthropologist, asked me what I do. 'What *is* social anthropology?', they have asked. The sorts of answers they have been looking for are rather varied. Some of them have wanted to know how social anthropology, as a branch of knowledge, relates to others like sociology, archaeology or human biology. Often the easiest way to answer that kind of question is to explain what social anthropology is not. The first chapter takes this as its theme, setting the subject in the context of other disciplines concerned with the study of humanity. In the process it tries to correct some of the misapprehensions that have accumulated over the rather short time that social anthropology has existed as a separate discipline.

Those who are thinking of going to university and who are not sure what subjects to choose, or the people who advise them, need a different answer. They want to know the range of ideas, the sort of information and the conclusions that characterize social anthropology, and whether it is the sort of intellectual activity to spend three years immersed in. They, like many others, have had their curiosity awakened by mention of the subject in the press, on television or in conversation. Others know that social anthropology is interested in peoples who live in exotic parts of the world, but how and why they are not sure. They would like to know what social anthropologists study, how they think and whether their ideas have any practical use. Chapter 2 addresses this sort of question; it sketches the outlines of the subject, indicating its scope, how researchers collect material and the way they formulate their ideas. The chapter is not a miniature textbook, although it would be helpful to read it before filling in an UCCA form or going for a university interview. It is designed to be read as complete in itself, but it could be the preliminary step towards a more prolonged study. Appendix A gives a list of books to help those who wish to take the subject a bit further by their own reading.

Parents and teachers want to be able to advise their children or pupils and share their interests. The book may be useful for them, particularly as Chapter 3 also discusses the uses of social anthropology. It considers how the subject trains one to think in particular ways and how this is useful in certain sorts of careers. Since social anthropology is very little taught in schools, few people have much idea of how it relates to school subjects, so this chapter also indicates which subjects form a useful background to social anthropology as a university course and how one can tell if it might suit someone to study it.

Of course, not everyone who is interested in social anthropology will want to concentrate on it alone, or even to take it as a degree course. This book is not only for those who are choosing university degree courses but who are considering subsidiary subjects or are thinking of taking evening classes. Social anthropology is taught with a wide variety of other subjects and can be studied at various levels. Appendix B gives a list of the universities where it is taught and the subjects it is combined with.

Social anthropology has been developing very rapidly in the last thirty years; today there are a number of different approaches contained within the discipline as a whole. This book represents my own view. Many of my colleagues would put more emphasis on some aspects than I have done, and less on others, giving a rather different picture of the whole. But often the controversies are technical and more specialized than is necessary here. I have not thought it helpful to argue my own case against opposing views but I think that most social anthropologists in Britain would find the book useful as a basis from which to develop their own theoretical position in more detail.

In writing it, I have been helped by memories of many conversations in which questions about social anthropology were raised. I am grateful to the people involved in them and also to Ginny Sackur and my publishers who read drafts of the book and made helpful suggestions. I owe warm thanks to Joan Wells, who typed a chaotic manuscript at record speed.

Social anthropology has absorbed my interest ever since I chose to study it without really knowing what it entailed. The purpose of this book is to help others make a more informed choice, but I hope very much that it also conveys some of the endless fascination of this particular way of understanding the world.

# 1

## What Social Anthropology is not

Twenty or thirty years ago, it would hardly have been necessary to start a book on social anthropology with a chapter like this. One could have begun, positively, with the subject itself. Very few people knew anything about it at all, what it studied, what its methods and conclusions were. There were very few universities where it could be studied for a degree and most social anthropologists were academics, whose work was known mainly to the other academics with whom they came in contact. There were no general books on the subject; the published work of social anthropologists was largely read by specialists. The small number of students had come across the subject more or less by accident; when asked by friends or relations what they were reading at university, the answer 'social anthropology' would usually have met blank faces or puzzled looks.

The situation is now very different, but it is also more confused. There is a general awareness that the subject exists, although it is still not normally taught in schools and most people have only rather vague impressions of what it is about. Some books for the general reader are available but most do not stay in print long. Despite the expansion of university education in the 1960s, which increased the teaching of social sciences in particular, few public libraries have staff who know much about social anthropology; if there *is* a section on social anthropology, it may contain a very odd assortment of titles. The works of Margaret Mead, for example, are out of date and even misleading, but they often form the sole basis of people's knowledge of the subject. Appendix A gives some suggestions for reading which is sounder and more up to date.

There are other sources of confusion as well. Television

programmes and articles in the colour supplements of news-papers and in magazines have introduced the public to a wide variety of exotic ways of living. The peoples of what is now called the Third World and their problems have become much more familiar to a much larger number of people. The experts on these areas are usually social anthropologists, whose work thus receives some publicity without adding much more to what is known about it. Since the mass media habitually deal with the unusual and surprising aspects of these societies and with scenes which are beautiful or startling, they perpetuate the mistaken idea that social anthropology is mainly concerned with 'primitive peoples', whose colourful existence is threat-ened by the spread of Western civilization. This is quite wrong, but the media cannot be blamed for introducing the idea. Pro-grammes like these are popular because they fit in with general misconceptions about the development of the world's human populations and the overall direction of history.

The inaccurate notions which are still current resemble ideas which were held by scholars in the nineteenth century. In those days the term anthropology meant any study of man, whatever aspect it dealt with. Social anthropology as a distinct field of enquiry really only dates from the first quarter of this century. The distinctions between it and other, related, disciplines are comparatively recent and often technical; for both these rea-sons they are little known and not understood. There is much greater familiarity with the older ideas which have become part of general knowledge. But few people have any inkling that those ideas have long since been found to be based on false assumptions or disproved by further study and better informa-tion. The publication of misleading popular works, by non-specialists, such as Robert Ardrey's *The Territorial Imperative*, further confuses the whole issue by offering explanations which are based on an imperfect knowledge of the several disciplines which the authors are bringing together. Books which do not claim to explain so much and confine themselves to expounding subjects which the authors have expert knowl-edge of may be less eye-catching but are usually better value. Paradoxically, the growth of general knowledge and the spread of ideas has made it more rather than less essential to start by making clear what social anthropology is not and to combat mistaken ideas about is conclusions.

## The human sciences

The label 'anthropology' belongs, strictly speaking, to two
separate branches of the study: physical and social anthropology. While the two have been distinct for a hundred years or
more, the common name still links them together. Physical
anthropologists are justifiably irritated by the modern practice
of using 'anthropology' to mean social anthropology; this
usage, which is largely confined to Britain, reflects the greater
expansion of social anthropology. In Europe 'anthropology'
is used to mean physical anthropology, while social anthropology is known under the name 'ethnology'. Since this book is
concerned with social anthropology, there should be no confusion if 'anthropology' appears on its own, as the full title is
rather clumsy; physical anthropology will always be clearly
indicated as such.

*Physical anthropology*  The subject matter of physical
anthropology is the species, *homo sapiens*. Physical anthropology has several branches, of which the best-known is probably human palaeontology. It is concerned with the evolution
of our species and early forms of the genus *homo*, and their
relation both to modern man and related mammals, such as
the great apes. It uses some of the same methods as archaeology to study the fossil record, using modern methods to date
the finds, most of which are fragmentary. Discoveries in
Africa, like those made by the Leakeys, have immensely complicated the family tree which was once thought to have linked
human ancestors with those of the great apes. It has length-
ened still more the span of time over which evolution must
have been taking place; the period for which we have good
evidence of how people lived is minute in comparison.

Other branches of physical anthropology are concerned
with the non-historical study of human physical variation, or
with trying to determine what distinguishes human beings
from the other mammals which they resemble. The study of
communication among the great apes, their social life and
behaviour is part of the attempt to understand what, if any,
are the physical universals which limit and shape social and
cultural behaviour. In this, physical anthropology relates the
sciences of zoology and biology to the social sciences, drawing
more on the findings of human biology and genetics perhaps,

than on the social sciences, but still linking the two.

It cannot be stressed too strongly, or too often, that physical anthropologists are not concerned with the study of 'race' and, indeed, reject the concept as having no scientific validity. Physical appearance is the result of numerous and complex structures of genes, whose distribution does not coincide with any socially or geographically distinct population. There is as much variation within any population as between different groups of people. All communities are so mixed in physical, intellectual and emotional dispositions that their individual members differ considerably among themselves, and their behaviour is the result of social rather than inherited factors. No evidence has been produced that would link the inherited make-up of any set of people with their behaviour or aptitudes. Indeed, each human being is unique in his or her genetic pattern. Recently a technique has been invented to make prints of these patterns which will be as individual as finger prints.

Race is now studied as a social stereotype, by social anthropologists interested in the way cultures use a selection of physical and other characteristics to define categories of people. Gender (sexual identity), age and parentage are other ideas of the same sort. A less significant example is the idea that red-haired people are hot-tempered, which is perpetuated despite many people knowing gentle, sweet-natured individuals who happen to have red hair. A consciousness of common origin can also serve to unite people in a common cause or to exclude others from access to scarce goods, opportunities or powerful positions. The nature and significance of these ideas vary from society to society and in one society over a period of time, so that it is clear that what is involved is determined by social factors. Hence the study of race relations lies within the province of social, rather than physical, anthropology.

While physical anthropology has one branch concerned with the past and others interested in contemporary human variation, social anthropology is not similarly divided. Where there are adequate written records of the past, we are talking about history, a much older discipline with methods of its own. Many of the peoples studied by social anthropologists have no written history, although they may have legends and traditions about past times. These are rather difficult for historians to use: either they are shaped by current preoccupations, ideas of what the past should have been, or are too general or fragmentary to be really helpful. Recently, however, historians of traditionally non-literate peoples have made new discoveries of source materials and learnt new techniques of interpretation, so that African history, for example, has become an established branch of history.

***The study of the past*** The question of the relation between anthropology and history has been a matter of some debate in anthropology. The debate is not so much about whether anthropologists should take into account the history of the peoples they study, where it is known, although that, too, is a matter of opinion. Rather, it is the question of whether the main aim should be to provide a generalized theory of social change, as distinct from the interpretation of past events, in a particular place. The debate is still a live issue and there are various different views, but it would be generally agreed that no satisfactory theory of social change has been developed yet. Social anthropology is concerned with the comparative analysis of social systems, while history seeks to understand the relations of past events to one another. Neither subject tries to answer the question 'why are people different?', if by that is meant 'how did it all begin?' The origins of human variation lie so far back in time as to be virtually beyond our knowledge.

Some historians have made good use of social anthropology as a guide to their own work. Studies of witchcraft in sixteenth century England or in early Rome have been stimulated by the work of anthropologists on this subject. A book by a group of Cambridge historians on European marriage and household structure in earlier times, and another on inheritance, have clearly been stimulated by what social anthropologists have to say about the connection between marriage patterns and property rights. Social anthropology is relevant to the work of historians because it points to connections between different aspects of social life in interpretations which historians find interesting, and not because modern societies resemble medieval or ancient Europe. In exchange, the work of African historians, for example, has contributed a good deal to improving the accuracy of anthropological work in the present, by providing an understanding of what happened in the past.

Archaeologists and prehistorians also study the past, but their evidence consists of the material remains of past societies. While the distinction between archaeology and history is clear in principle, in practice historians and archaeologists contribute to one another's work on periods, like that of classical Greece and Rome, where there are both written records and material objects to study. The prehistorians, as their name implies, work on periods before written records exist. They, like archaeologists and palaeontologists, use excavation to discover evidence for what happened, often far back in time, and have developed sophisticated techniques for preserving and dating what they find. Archaeologists are more cautious today about generalizing on the whole of human history from what they know about changes in just one particular site than they used to be in the past. At that time it was thought that the societies studied by archaeologists resembled the living peoples studied by social anthropologists so closely that one could treat the existing societies as survivals from the past.

Today the relationship between archaeology, including prehistory, and social anthropology is much less close. While the ethnographic studies of social anthropologists may be used to interpret archaeological evidence, it is now recognized that there are dangers in doing so. One can say, for example, that at one time all the peoples of the world obtained their food by hunting and gathering; it is much less easy to use what is known about societies which do this today to add to our understanding of the distant past. Modern peoples who live by hunting and gathering vary very considerably in how they organize society, in their beliefs and even in the way they exploit their food supply; there is no necessary connection between how people obtain their food and what their social life is like. The prehistorians have little evidence of this aspect of the lives of peoples who lived without writing, so it is impossible to decide which of the modern peoples resemble these ancient societies, if any.

Take the important matter of estimating the population of a prehistoric community as an example: one cannot deduce much either from the number of camp-sites in an area or the availability of its food supplies. Anthropological studies in Africa and Asia have shown that a group of 15 or 20 people may make as many as a hundred camps in a year, since they move every two or three days and the group constantly changes membership, some moving away and others joining it. These moves depend on a lot of factors, such as how people are getting on together, whether there has been illness or death in the camp and even whether moving is considered a good thing to do. The availability of food supplies is only one of several considerations. By contrast there are other societies, described in the recent past, who lived in semi-permanent villages but moved to temporary camps during certain fishing seasons. Similar differences in styles of living probably existed in the distant past so that comparisons between the past and the present are pretty speculative. On balance, most social anthropologists probably think that the use made by prehistorians and archaeologists of their material does little more than underline the fact that we can know very little about the remote past, and are often reduced to guesswork.

***Comparative technology***   The modern study which relates most closely to archaeology is known as material culture or comparative technology. This is the study of the material aspect of a people's culture, the things they make to use, ritual objects, arts and other skills. It may include a study of the introduction of new objects and techniques from other societies, and the development of skills over time. It has developed very rapidly from the study of the distribution of different objects, which was part of the early-twentieth-century attempt to establish a global history of mankind. Its work relates to that of social anthropology but is closer to some forms of ethnology in Europe, which have not specialized as much in the social side of human variation as social anthropology has done in Britain. It is also, of course, associated with the work of museums of ethnography, like the Museum of Mankind in London, which is part of the British Museum.

The human sciences – physical anthropology, palaeontology, history, archaeology, prehistory and material culture – are quite distinct from social anthropology, but they share a common origin and a general interest in understanding all aspects of human life. Moreover, they share the conviction that it is only by careful study of all the available evidence that valid conclusions can be reached. They differ in the problems they seek to solve and the methods of study they have developed. Individual scholars do cross the boundaries, which have been emphasized here to show the differences between all these disciplines and social anthropology; where a piece of work seeks to combine two approaches to a problem, the research must make clear how this is being done, for specialists on both sides will be concerned to see that they are satisfied. Much of what passes for anthropology in the popular works of today is spoiled from the beginning by ignorance of the specialized subjects which are being included in a hodgepodge of ideas drawn from a number of them.

## Some popular misconceptions

The last hundred years or so has produced such an explosion of knowledge and proliferation of specializations that it has become virtually impossible for even the most dedicated and intelligent layman to keep up with the latest advances. This is particularly so in the social and human sciences, which were in their infancy in the nineteenth century. Most of what has been described here as distinct subjects was included then in a general 'science of man'. This early anthropology showed some signs of the specialization to come but mostly failed to distinguish clearly between past and present, physical or social, material or immaterial aspect of human life. The work was integrated by the theory of human evolution, which dominated it for nearly a century. It is sometimes thought that this theory was taken from Darwin's work on the evolution of species in plants and animals, but that is not accurate. Darwin's work, like that of others who expounded evolutionary theory, before and after him, is best seen as a manifestation of the general Victorian belief in progress. Although this view had its roots in earlier ideas, it was greatly strengthened by the technological advances of the Industrial Revolution, which seemed to confirm the power of the newly established sciences, not only to explain the world but to transform it.

In the course of their development, the sciences of man discarded evolutionism. Unfortunately, however, it remains entrenched in general knowledge, which has not yet been greatly influenced by the developments in the human sciences of this century. In addition, Western society, like all societies, operates on certain myths about its own relation to other peoples, which form part of a general framework for understanding the world. They are still to be found in popular writing as well as in the work of scholars for they involve basic assumptions about human nature. Two in particular are relevant to this discussion; one because it continues to support an idea of progress and the other because it represents the directly opposite view. One can call them myths because they derive from, and justify, widely held views of our own society and they are often held despite the existence of evidence to the contrary. They are moral judgements, evaluations of better or worse, which support popular misconceptions of what anthropology is and does.

*Social order* The first myth sees society as the imposition of law and order on human beings whose nature is to be self-seeking and aggressive. The view is essentially the same as that implied by the Christian doctrine of original sin. Social order is obtained by control of the individual, and such peace allows the accumulation of wisdom, riches and the improvement of life for all. When elaborated into a belief that humanity is progressing from a state of savage nature towards greater civilization, the myth provides an optimistic view of social evolution. Naturally, it was this view which supported the Victorian conviction that with the development of science and improved technology would come improved versions of society.

*The noble savage* The opposite myth can also be found in Christian thought, but in the Book of Genesis in the Bible. It can be called the myth of 'the noble savage'; in it, social life itself is held responsible for conflict, injustice and disharmony in social life. This view, which has undoubtedly influenced many reformers and revolutionaries, including leaders of the French Revolution, sees 'simple' society as a peaceful existence in accord with nature. A more recent version of it is implicit in the ideas of those who attribute all social evils to modern society, to the over-development of technology and the ever-increasing production of material goods. An interest in simple or exotic societies may be motivated by a desire to find an alternative way of life that will lead to happiness.

The two myths can be seen in the conclusions drawn from the first comparisons made between other societies and our own, the earliest attempts to understand the nature of social life and its variety. However, neither view is confirmed by the work of social anthropology; both are over-simplified and crude. All societies show both conflict and cooperation, all human beings have the same capacities for greed or for altruism. Modern social anthropology does its best to keep free of all moral evaluations. It is not possible to evaluate whole societies as 'better' or 'worse' so a brief example will serve to show. Some of the small isolated peoples of Africa live in apparent harmony because when there is a quarrel or a conflict of interests, the individuals concerned separate, going to live with different groups for a while. This sounds like an admirable social system. Yet in the very same societies, infants may be killed at birth or the sick and elderly may be left behind when a group moves to its next camp. Such practices seem the opposite of admirable to us, but they and the lack of fighting are all products of a system in which social ties are fragile. To attempt to label such a society as better or worse than our own is misguided; worse still, it impedes our understanding. This means, of course, that social anthropology cannot find a blueprint for peace and happiness by searching through varied social forms for the ideal one. Just because the subject has accumulated a store of information about the varied ways in which human beings live together, it does not hold the key to human happiness.

*Social evolution*   However, it is the contrary belief, that there *is* a continual progress in human social arrangements, that is the more influential today, as it was in the nineteenth century. While people may not be very clear about what evolutionism was, they still accept many of its conclusions. In order to clear away these misconceptions we will first have to consider the theory itself. Social evolutionism, as distinct from the biological evolutionary theory developed by Darwin, was based on the identification of simple forms with early ones. Believing that the general trend of evolution in society was from simple forms of society to more complex ones, they assumed that the simple societies still in existence were identical with the early stages of all mankind's development. They were thought to be, so to speak, living fossils, having developed so far and no further. By arranging known societies on the scale from most simple to most complex, the history of the human race could be understood, or so they thought. The yardstick for measuring any particular people's place on the ladder of progress was the same as that used by the archaeologists: the method of obtaining food and the level of material sophistication. Gathering nuts, berries and wild vegetables and hunting wild animals was the earliest type of economy and changes were associated with 'inventions': of agriculture, pottery, metal-working or writing. Other aspects of social life such as forms of marriage or government, religious beliefs or ideas about inheritance were assumed to be associated with the different material stages. The evolutionists did not expect to find living examples of the very earliest societies, so they felt free to deduce logically what these must have been. Looking back on their work a century later, we can see that what they often did was to assume that the earliest known society was the opposite of their own. So they generally agreed that the first human societies had no conception of marriage but lived in a state of sexual promiscuity, with no one knowing or caring about links between parents and children. Life-long monogamy was believed to be the latest and 'best' stage of development, the basis for the Christian family. So promiscuity was associated with early humanity and the various marriage and family arrangements of other societies ordered in between the two extremes. Various schemes for the evolution of social institutions were constructed by different scholars according to their own particular interests in law, religion or marriage. They used their knowledge of ancient Greece and Rome to help in their comparisons; since what they were concerned with was the development of 'civilization' they did not think accurate chronology was necessary. What was important was the stage of development of a society, not the period in time at which it existed.

While there was general agreement about evolution in general terms, opinions differed about how it happened. There were fierce arguments about whether the social recognition of maternal or paternal identity came first, and arguments about what were the key institutions in understanding the course of evolution. It was mainly library work, for very few of these early anthropologists had personal experience of any of the societies they studied. Indeed, when Sir James Frazer, author of the massive work on religion, *The Golden Bough*, was asked if he had ever known a 'native', Frazer exclaimed 'But Heaven forbid'.

Evolutionism left its marks on social anthropology; while rejecting the general theory, a later generation of anthropologists continued to use the comparative method, though for other purposes. An emphasis on the study of simple societies has also been characteristic of anthropology, although it has never restricted its attention to them, and of course the use of comparison emphasized the concern with all forms of society. But evolutionary theory was based on a number of assumptions which have been shown to be quite wrong. The first was to assume that all aspects of society can be deduced from a knowledge of productive techniques, or indeed any other institution. There are still a number of peoples in the world who do not cultivate or possess domesticated animals. In all other respects they vary very considerably. The Hadza of Tanzania have rather vague religious beliefs and simple religious ceremonies, while the Australian aboriginees possess complicated religious myths and perform elaborate rituals. The Bushmen of the Kalahari live in simply-organized communities; people are free to change the group they live with and often do so, while among the peoples of the North-west Coast of America, in an area which is now divided between the United States and Canada, the hunting and gathering economy of the different tribes accompanied an elaborate system of clans and hereditary ranks. Since all that survives of the distant past for a prehistorian to uncover are the material aspects of a people's life, we cannot know what our earliest forebears thought, or how they organized their communities. Obviously, then, we cannot know whether or not they resemble modern societies, and if they do, which. All the societies in the world have had the same length of time in which to evolve. The complex mythologies or marriage rules which characterize some modern peoples whose technology is very simple, are likely to be the result of their own long histories. The fundamental equation between simple and early, on which evolutionism was based, cannot be sustained.

To succeed as an explanation, evolutionism would have had to explain why some societies continued to evolve and why others did not. This it has never done satisfactorily. Isolation of some peoples cannot be the answer as there is now evidence to show much more contact between peoples and large-scale movements of population in many parts of the world. Recent discoveries of complex societies in many parts of the world, which have collapsed and disappeared makes it clear that our knowledge of the past is still very incomplete. Archaeological work in Central America has made it clear that the Mayan civilization extended much further back in time than was previously thought; the archaeology of China is still in its infancy and the ruins of Zimbabwe are not yet completely understood in the context of Central African history as a whole. It is far more in accord with the information we do have to conclude that all societies have been continually changing and adapting to changes thrust upon them, than that some did so, and others did not. Moreover, the evolutionist view was sometimes coupled with an implicit idea that certain peoples were inherently more gifted with potential then others, a view which has been found to be completely unfounded. The racist implications of evolutionary thinking were not accepted by all scholars even then and, by the end of the nineteenth century, the study of social and cultural life has been distinguished from the study of human biology. Without any explanation for the unevenness of development in different societies, evolutionism as a theory was too weak to survive.

Evolutionism has been discussed at length because it is the source of many inaccurate ideas, both about the societies studied by anthropologists and about the subject's aims in studying them. Journalists still use the epithet 'stone-age' about remote and simple societies, implying that they represent what our own earliest ancestors must have been like. Some of these outmoded ideas are also used to bolster prejudice, so it is important to be emphatic that modern social anthropology is not a theory of evolution.

***Exotic lives***  Social anthropology is not exclusively concerned with exotic or 'primitive peoples', although much of its research has been done among them. The subject grew from the desire to understand why human beliefs and behaviour differed so widely across the world and through history; the ultimate goal was to define the essentials of human nature, underneath the various social guises they assumed. The comparative method was designed to distinguish invariant, presumed universal, features from those which could be shown to vary. The concentration on simple societies was the result of the belief that the task of understanding the workings of simple forms was easier and should precede the study of more complex ones. The more that emphasis was put on the interrelation of parts of social systems within a whole, the greater advantage there seemed to be in studying societies which were structurally simple and culturally homogeneous so that they could be directly observed as working wholes. Moreover, observations made among people very unlike members of one's own society are more likely to cover everything, without taking anything for granted, since everything seems fresh in its strangeness. However, the aim remains comparative, and some social anthropologists have worked in complex, industrial societies, and not only in recent years. A survey of anthropological work in the Mediterranean lists over 200 authors in the bibliography and cites work going back nearly a hundred years.

Social anthropologists cannot be said to be 'interested in people', either, if by that is meant the feelings, ideas and motives of individuals. The social consists of what is general in a community, or part of one, although it is true that it must be established through talking to individual members of the group, observing their behaviour and listening to them talk among themselves. In studying the Gisu, an agricultural people in eastern Uganda, it was easy to get anyone to describe the relationship that should exist between fathers and their sons. Fathers were expected to be responsible for their sons' actions until they were fully adult (which meant when they were initiated) to support them, pay what was necessary for the initiation ceremonies and for marriage, handing over to them sufficient land to build a homestead and cultivate the crops necessary to support a family. Sons should be respectful and obedient to their fathers, loyal and prepared to follow advice when it was offered. Another strand in their relationship concerned the fact that a dead father became an ancestor with power to affect the future of his descendants and that without such descendants no man achieved the summit of his ambition. The reality was that relations between fathers and sons were often full of tension; quarrels broke out, leading in some cases to fights and, in a very few cases, to a man being killed by his son. Gisu would discuss particular cases in terms, either of the personalities involved, or by reference to their moral code: so-and-so was a bad father or somebody else an ungrateful ne'er do well son. They explained each case separately as a deviation from what was normal or proper. In extreme cases they assumed that the persons concerned were either mad or drunk, that is, abnormal. Psychological explanations are also individual ones, but of a different sort; they concern the emotional organization of the individuals concerned, and depend on information about feelings, or states of mind. By contrast, the social anthropologist must look for how the relationship between father and son affects and is affected by, other social institutions; in this case, property, the political system, marriage patterns. The final explanation did not explain why particular individuals had assaulted or killed their fathers, while others had not. It aimed to show how the ideal of father/son harmony was affected by the fact that the relationship did not exist in isolation but as part of the total social system. This example serves to show that what social anthropology is interested in is society, not 'people'. Some of those who come to study it, do so under the mistaken impression that it will provide complete explanations why individuals behave as they do. It may then be disappointing to discover the rather formal, abstract terms in which behaviour is discussed by anthropologists. It is as well to be clear from the outset that, while social anthropology can throw a good deal of fresh light on behaviour, it is primarily concerned with what it reveals of the social system.

*Not sociology*    Sociology also studies society; indeed, some scholars have considered social anthropology to be merely a branch of sociology. It has been described as 'sociology in tents', as though the only difference between the two subjects was a question of subject matter. It does sometimes appear as though the distinction is merely a division of labour, with sociologists studying large, industrial societies, while the non-industrial world is left to social anthropologists. The joking reference to tents is, of course, an allusion to this. But like many jokes, it is only partly true. While sociology and social anthropology have several intellectual ancestors in common and share some of the same concepts, social anthropology is not, to my mind, sociology. The divergence is a matter of interests: sociologists are concerned both with society in the abstract and also with studies of particular institutions. They have tended to balance uneasily between social philosophy on the one hand and social engineering on the other; much of what is written by sociologists is either at a very high level of abstractness or more or less directly connected with social problems. Anthropology has, until recently, maintained its distance from the solution of practical problems and, being based in the comparison of particular societies, avoids formal theory, insisting on the verification of generalizations by research rather than logic.

The methods of sociology and social anthropology are rather different; sociology uses the questionnaire and formal interviews as well as documentary evidence, including statistics. The characteristic method of social anthropology is what is known as participant observation, which essentially means direct observation, living with the community being studied and learning to speak its language. More social anthropologists have begun to use sociological methods for particular research problems which require quantitative analysis and some sociologists use participant observation. There is convergence as well as divergence. However, the distinctive feature of social anthropology lies in none of these features but in the fact that it is comparative. It is the concern to relate the concepts, symbols and thought of a people to the structure of their society, to understand their thoughts as well as their behaviour which is crucially different from sociology.

Social anthropology has been called the child of colonialism. Those who use such a phrase intend it to imply a number of different reasons why the findings of the previous generations of social anthropologists should be discounted. They argue that social anthropology as a subject of enquiry arose out of the requirements of the dominant white colonizers to control their subject peoples in the Third World, and keep them subservient. This work was not only biased by this origin in general, but in particular it neglected to consider the changing nature of traditional societies, portraying them instead as static and lacking the potential for development.

This is a complicated controversy and one which generates strong feelings that only add to the confusion of the debate. The accusation mixes up a number of different issues which must be disentangled before they can be discussed. First, of course, there is an historical question: it is true that an interest in peoples very different from those in Europe was stimulated by contacts with them and that these contacts were the results of the expansion of Europe, starting in the sixteenth century. It is true too that the social sciences, including social anthropology, developed rapidly in the nineteenth century. But this period was characterized by rapid social and economic change in Europe, the effects of the gathering momentum of the Industrial Revolution and not merely by the increase in overseas empires, so that one cannot attribute this development solely to one or the other. Most of what is now recognizable as social anthropology is the product of the middle of the twentieth century when the colonial empires were beginning to crumble. Historically, it is a bit dubious to attribute social anthropology's origins to colonialism.

Secondly, while the voyages of exploration and later expeditions and field researches were financed by rulers and, later, governments who may well have done so for political and economic motives, the explorers themselves seem often to have acted out of the desire to find out about the world and make a name for themselves by the discovery of new marvels. It is not unknown even now for scientific research to be presented to funding agencies as being useful to them. We should distinguish both between the intentions of different sorts of people involved and also between their aims and the effects of their actions which might only be understood with hindsight.

The most important issue raised by this controversy is the question of whether a body of knowledge can ever be objective in the sense of being independent of the society that produced it or of the interests of its ruling class. Those who argue that social anthropology is determined by its origins must also accept that any other theory, including their own, is similarly affected. If social anthropology is the child of the imperialist capitalism of the nineteenth century, then so is Marxism. If all knowledge is merely the product of a particular society then the logical conclusion is that objective truth is a mirage and all scholarship is biased, surely a counsel of despair.

However, it is not necessary to take this position. The founders of the social sciences, and in particular those who were interested in comparing societies, were most often critics of the dominant ideas of their time, rather than apologists for its élite. A tradition of independent thinking runs from the scholars of the Enlightenment, who challenged the authority of religious dogma, through the nineteenth-century scholars, who believed in the inevitability of progress, to the social anthropologists of the mid twentieth century, who saw themselves as spokesmen for the peoples they knew against the colonial authorities and missionaries, who were trying to change them. This is not surprising, for large, complex societies are differentiated into numerous sub-groups with different relations to the centres of power; it is they who produce ideas which may challenge the dominant ideology and who, ultimately, may change it.

Social anthropology is not – in my view – a child of, or a justification for, colonialism or white domination. While it evolved within a certain type of society, its aim is to compare and to strive, as far as possible, for the objective view. It is no longer the study of humanity in every aspect, but only of social life. It is not the study of human biology, nor human physical evolution, subjects which are studied by physical anthropology; it is not the study of the human past which is the province of history, archaeology and palaeontology; nor is it the study of social evolution or the collection of exotic customs practised in remote corners of the world; it resembles sociology, but it is not sociology abroad any more than sociology is social anthropology at home. Now, having tried to clear away some of the misconceptions which surround the subject, it is high time to turn to what social anthropology is.

# 2

## What Social Anthropology is

Perhaps the best known fact about social anthropologists is that they usually do research by going abroad, to live in some exotic places. What is much less well understood is why they do it. This form of research is usually referred to as field-work, by analogy with the field studies of the natural sciences or geography. Its first aim is to provide as complete a description as possible of a particular people. Field-workers will usually have some technical problems in which they are interested, but they will always be studied as part of a total system. The second objective is to compare the system, or parts of it, with others, relating the analysis to a general body of knowledge about society, testing previous conclusions and thus hoping to advance our understanding further. Each piece of research is thus part of social anthropology as a whole, and is not merely a way of recording quaint customs and unusual ways of life, as if for an encyclopaedia of human behaviour. Ideas which have been developed in previous research are tested in field-work as well as new ones formulated; field research is an exacting piece of hard work, not merely an interesting experience of living in a foreign place, though it may be that as well.

This chapter will start from social anthropology's distinctive method, which is known as participant observation. It will cover, briefly, the main areas of social life: economics, politics, kinship and religion, indicating the general scope of present knowledge and some current matters of discussion. In the course of this, it will be necessary to give brief definitions of some main concepts: social function, social structure and culture, which are technical terms in social anthropology; and also the notion of ethnocentricity, which is the word used for the subject's central dilemma: that we are all, social anthropologists included, members of a particular society and this must influence the way we think about other societies.

## Field-work as a method of research

Participant observation means the observation of social life, as far as possible from within, that is, at firsthand; but it is also designed as a method of research, to obtain systematic information. It entails living in a community as much like everyone else in the community as possible. Research consists of listening to conversations, quarrels and discussions, as well as asking questions, observing what people do as well as what they say should be done and what they think of other people's behaviour. In a sense, the field-worker begins by becoming like a child learning the language and how to behave properly. It involves learning the appropriate greetings, how to eat and sit politely (not always an easy matter for those who are accustomed to chairs, knives and forks), and gradually coming to understand the implicit meanings which underlie what the people themselves can explain about their way of living and thinking. The process is very much quicker than a child's learning, of course; it is also designed to collect specific information.

Participant observation is supplemented by maps, and sets of figures which are used to discover regularities in social life: the average size of herds, numbers of people in the households and so on. The songs and prayers which form part of ceremonies are recorded, as well as family trees, historical traditions and sacred myths. A daily record of events, notes on conversations and personalities is essential. The information collected on one trip may take years to analyse and write up.

*Understanding through language*   The essential tool of field-work is a thorough command of the language, or languages, spoken in the community. This may not be easy to acquire, since other languages use sounds and constructions which are very different from the European languages most fieldworkers were brought up to speak. Many of the peoples studied by social anthropologists speak languages that are not written down; there are no grammars or dictionaries to consult. Learning the language of a very remote community may entail learning another language first, or a lingua franca, in order to communicate with anyone at all. The reader may well wonder whether it would not be better just to find an interpreter to translate everything, rather than adding to the difficulty of the work by learning the language first.

Knowledge of a language gives one access to information about a people that cannot be obtained in any other way. To begin with, the language itself carries clues to the mental world of the people who speak it. The vocabulary indicates the range and direction of their concern with the world around them, and their own way of life. Evans-Pritchard, who studied the pastoral Nuer of the Sudan, estimated that their language had several thousand words referring to cattle: several hundred colour terms, others denoting the shape of horns, the age and sex of the animals and so forth. There are also figurative uses of terms and poetic images; in all an impressive demonstration of what Evans-Pritchard called 'an obsession' with cattle. He did not mean this literally, of course; cattle have a vital economic importance to the Nuer. English shows a similar proliferation of slang terms for money!

The distinctions made between classes of things and people also reflect a particular view of reality; indeed, one such set of terms, which is found in all societies, is an important field of study in itself: these are the terms applied to relatives and to people related by marriage, described as a kinship terminology. The terms form a system, providing a framework for understanding a set of social relationships that have very great significance in any society.

The way in which people use their language tells one as much as the language itself; those who speak it as their mother tongue very often do not recognize the patterns of usage that develop. During my first field-work, I was once asked by a foreign teacher the meaning of a term which Gisu schoolboys used to each other; it was the term for brother-in-law. When I asked my Gisu neighbours about this they told me there must be some marriage link between the boys' families. Continuing to listen for the word, I found it used between business partners, between buyers and sellers in the market and in a number of different contexts. It became clear that the word was used as the English use 'mate', a friendly term between people who know each other and are on terms of equality. The usage made me examine the relation of brothers-in-law more closely and gave me a better understanding of a whole range of ideas about friendship, equality and personal relations, which I might never have noticed if I had been using an interpreter in a formal interview.

The ability to understand spontaneous conversations, rather than relying solely on question and answer, gives a far better sense of how a society works than the answers to any questions. Gossip, arguments and full-scale rows reveal how the ideals of conduct work out in practice, how political followings are built up, reputations won and lost, or children taught to behave. Once, when I was in bed with some illness, I overheard a conversation between two old women discussing whether my illness could be due to witchcraft or not. It gave me a valuable insights into not only what they thought about my illness, but about white people and the possibility of their 'becoming Gisu'; I am sure they would not have said the same things to my face.

In any society, much of the meaning conveyed by speech comes from an understanding of its context, the whole situation in which it is used. It was Malinowski, one of the founders of modern social anthropology, who first showed this. He was perhaps the greatest exponent of intensive field-work, which he pioneered in his own work, in the Trobriand Islands off the coast of New Guinea. His book *Argonauts of the Western Pacific* is a study of the exchange of shell ornaments. It shows how the significance of this exchange leads one into a consideration of craftsmanship, agriculture, magic, leadership and wealth: in short, the exchange only makes sense in the context of Trobriand culture as a whole. In the other monographs he published on different aspects of Trobriand social life, he showed the complexity of understandings which were required to interpret what was said and done in different situations.

*Observation*    Language, however valuable, is only part of field-work. The other part is the observation of the pattern of events and activities which make up the annual calendar. In many parts of the world, social life is lived in public far more than it is in Europe, so that it is relatively easy to observe the daily life of a community. Indeed, one of the reasons why field-work in industrialized societies is so much more difficult is that people are not readily accessible to this sort of observation. Houses are built of more solid materials so that what goes on in them is less easily discoverable. Special care has to be taken to obtain material which is similar to that obtained in villages where the walls of houses are thin and much of life is lived outdoors. Moreover, there is a tendency on the part of observers to accept notions like the privacy of family life because they are part of the ideas taken for granted by the researchers as well. Social anthropologists who will not jib at probing into the most intimate areas of family life in societies which are strange to them are much less searching when it comes to studying people like themselves. Paradoxically, our knowledge of European communities is often more superficial, less satisfactory than that provided by ethnographic descriptions of other societies.

Other disciplines have found that they have much to gain by using similar methods. The 'natural experiment' used by some social psychologists entails observing social life in particular contexts, rather than conducting their research with artificially selected groups of people; economists, political scientists and other social scientists, particularly those interested in the Third World, have adapted the method to their own use, having learnt that direct questioning may not be an accurate guide to what people do, and may even bias the answer, while observation can provide a greater depth of understanding of the results obtained by other methods. Participant observation is a distinctive technique of research, not merely a method forced on social anthropology by the fact that the peoples they study live far away, in areas where more conventional methods cannot be used.

Formerly, social anthropologists found themselves in the position of being the only experts on 'their' particular peoples. They covered topics which in literate societies are the province of economists, lawyers, political scientists or scholars interested in religion, literature or history. In being thus forced to cover all aspects of social life, anthropology has often been able to demonstrate unexpected connections between institutions which, because they are studied by different kinds of people, are thought to be quite separate. Thus we might not think that witchcraft had much to do with law and order but anthropological studies of witchcraft have shown that beliefs in, and accusations of, witchcraft may have the effect of making people keep to their obligations and refrain from exploiting those weaker than themselves. We associate government with state institutions, but anthropologists have shown that societies without these institutions are not chaotic; they govern themselves in other ways. As a result of their wide coverage of all aspects of social life, anthropologists' work interests a whole range of other social scientists who are concerned with single aspects of larger, more complex industralized societies, such as economics, law, religion or 'the family'.

Today many of the places where social anthropologists do research are also studied by other experts. Social anthropologists who worked in the literate societies of India, the Middle East or Europe have always had to take into account the specialist work of Orientalists, Arabists or experts in the literature and theology of the peoples they were studying. Nowadays the small communities in which social anthropologists are interested are much more closely integrated into nation states. Increasingly, work is carried out in towns where the population is very mixed. (In some cases the whole nation, like Somalia, is composed of a single 'people'.) The studies of other social scientists, however, tend to focus on the large units, nations and regions and their findings may be more difficult to use at the grass-roots level where much anthropological field-work is done. But in general, most anthropologists can expect to find relevant works by others which will provide background or supplementary information to that obtained by anthropological methods.

Participant observation has been criticized for being 'unscientific'; by this people usually mean that it does not use the experimental methods of science or, more generally, that social anthropologists do not couch their generalizations in the form of scientific laws. Most anthropologists would probably argue that they do not pretend to be scientists. The difference between social sciences and other sciences is that the former study beings of the same nature as the research worker, who have opinions of their own about the work and often about the person who is doing it. The relationship between them makes the situation quite different from that of the biologist studying the behaviour of rats. It is possible for the personality of a field-worker, or the relationship between the worker and members of the community being studied, to bias the enquiry.

Professional anthropologists are trained to be aware of this; the first research is carried out under supervision and it is one of the tasks of the supervisor to point out areas where judgement does not seem to be objective. There is a well-known case of two American anthropologists who studied the same village and came to very different conclusions about it. The first described a village that 'chose progress', its people taking advantage of new opportunities opened up to them by social change. The second emphasized the conflicts and inequalities that seemed to him to be undermining a traditional way of life. Neither account is entirely satisfactory since the selection of information is obviously biased by these very different moral judgements. An even more striking example of this is to be seen in Colin Turnbull's study of the Mountain People where the author's own feelings colour his whole interpretation of what he observed.

An ethnographic description should be both systematic and coherent; conclusions must be supported by evidence and it is not difficult to spot inconsistencies. Social anthropologists aim to be professional about separating personal judgements from the analysis of data. If a piece of work is to contribute to a general understanding of society, it must conform to common standards of verification. Social anthropology may not be a science but that does not mean it lacks intellectual rigour.

The modern field-worker expects to collect some data in numerical form. However, it has been made abundantly clear that such material itself has a number of weaknesses, of which the chief one is that the way in which the data is collected may influence results. In many societies other than our own, people frequently eat and sleep in different households; visitors come and go, the food is provided by one set of people and eaten by a slightly different set. According to what one decides is the criterion for membership of a household, eating together, sleeping under the same roof or sharing the production or consumption of food, the results of a household survey may have different results. People may have strong objections to saying how many children or animals they have, for fear of attracting bad luck or the jealousy of their neighbours. In many parts of the world disease or death in childhood or from natural disasters are common enough for people not to feel sure that their children will grow up or their herds continue to prosper. Not surprisingly, they do not like to be asked to count their chickens before they are hatched.

Even where there are public records, the interpretation of figures may not be easy. The problem of estimating divorce rates has been the subject of considerable discussion, although where there are reliable court records it may look simple. A true divorce rate consists of the number of marriages which end in divorce. In order to estimate this one would have to wait until all the marriages made in any one year had ended, either through divorce or the death of one or both partners; but this would mean that the divorce rate for that year could not be discovered until about sixty years later. But people want to know the survival rate of current marriages, and policy-makers want to make estimates for the future, so some other way has to be found. The divorces granted in any particular year end marriages which began over a long period of years beforehand; they cannot be compared with the marriages which began in that year. There are figures to show how many years the marriages which ended in divorce lasted but none to say how many of those still existing will end in divorce in the future. Present practice is to calculate the divorce rate as a percentage of married people as the most accurate available method. However, where divorce is frequent, many people will be married more than once and other factors which affect the rate of marriage will also affect the final figure. The tendency for people to live together without getting married may reduce the number of married couples and so make the divorce rate seem higher; the lowering of the legal age of marriage to 16 increased the number of married people and had the opposite effect on the divorce rate. While the methods used to calculate divorce rates and compile other statistical information are increasingly sophisticated, they may unavoidably contain uncertainties which limit, more or less according to the methods used, the accuracy of the picture they present.

In states with highly organized bureaucracies, a large amount of statistical information is collected by public officials and made available to the researcher. This may not be the case in all parts of the world, or the figures may be very inaccurate. Anthropologists may have to collect basic information on population and resources themselves and weigh up the value of getting this quantifiable information against possible inaccuracies and the time it will take to get the figures. Opinions differ as to the importance of statistics in different research problems; some people rely more on this kind of data than others.

Another criticism of the method has been that it is really only suited to the study of small, isolated populations, such as those studied early in the subject's history. Participant observation does limit the size of the community that can be studied, since there is a limit to the number of people whom one can get to know well. Where they are members of a people that numbers tens of thousands or more, as is quite possible, how can anthropologists be sure that their conclusions apply throughout the whole society? In the case of a traditional kingdom, like the Lozi of Zambia, where subject peoples of differing origins were incorporated into the nation, this would seem to be a difficulty that can only be overcome by several studies. There has been a long-standing debate among social anthropologists who have studied India about the relation between studies based on certain castes and regions and generalizations about Hindu India as a whole, since the castes have different understandings of Hinduism, and regions differ quite markedly in some aspects of their social life.

The short answer to this criticism is that it mixes up several different problems. The size of a population is not a problem in itself; if it has a relatively uniform way of life, the general social principles discovered by the study of one small part will be widely generalizable. A nation which incorporates different peoples within itself without absorbing them completely will have a different structure. It will probably need to be studied by the technique advocated by Audrey Richards in her study of Ganda villages in Uganda. She argues that in a traditional state the principles of political life operating at the centre must be analysed in order to understand the structure of villages.

The choice of a place to do field-work is an important preliminary in any piece of research. Some problems can only be studied in a particular part of the world: one would go to India to study the caste system, but those interested in hunting and gathering societies may choose to go to a number of different areas of the world where such methods of obtaining food are still used. Most researchers specialize in one or two regions and in the particular aspects of society that they find most interesting, but these are not the only considerations which narrow the field of choice. Practical and political difficulties have also to be considered. Some countries may be suffering from natural disasters or internal upheavals which make a study of normal social life impossible. Others may ban research or impose conditions which make research too difficult. In Russia one is required to take an official 'interpreter' and long stays are not permitted; in South Africa the system of apartheid makes it impossible for a white social anthropologist to live in a black community to study it. Elsewhere there may be closed areas, or areas where research is reserved for nationals of the country concerned. Many governments require foreigners to obtain affiliation to a local research institute, or determine from them what research may be done. As a result of these and other factors much less research is done in Africa than was the case in the fifties and sixties, but some new areas, like New Guinea and lowland South America, have been opened up for study. The difficulties and cost of getting to do research in the more traditional areas of research is a contributory factor to the rapid increase of field-work in Europe. Eastern Europe has been relatively little studied by Western anthropologists as permission is hard to obtain and the costs are high. But field-work around the Mediterranean and in Europe generally has been well-established for years.

Field-work, in the sense of a year or more spent in a community studying some aspect of social life in depth, is a matter for those who are or hope to be, professional anthropologists. Some departments of social anthropology do give their undergraduates a taste of this experience by requiring them to write a long essay in their third year, for which they may do some independent research in the long vacation between their second and third years. With only a limited period available it is obvious that unless a student already has a good command of another language than English, the research will have to be limited to sections of British society. It is not easy to rid oneself of deep-seated assumptions about how the society that one lives in works and to study it objectively, so that undergraduate field-work is difficult and necessarily somewhat superficial. However, many students find some first-hand experience of relating data to theory fascinating and rewarding. Some departments consider that they have their work cut out just to teach an understanding of the general principles of social anthropology in three years, without time being taken up with research for an essay, and do not include this in their degree; still others have experimented with it and given it up. The opportunity to do field research is not essential to one's grasp of the subject, however, and is no guide to the quality of the degree that is being offered.

Finally, it should be emphasized, the aim of field research is the study of a social system and in particular a problem within the body of theory which constitutes the subject. It is no longer the attempt to describe a 'disappearing world'. Put in that context, the question of whether the community studied is representative no longer arises. Participant observation is a technique for studying social life in depth, not an illusion that one small section can represent a whole people or nation.

## The scope of anthropological enquiry

The peoples traditionally studied by social anthropologists used to be referred to as 'primitive', a word which originally referred to the simplicity of their social organization. However, the word carried overtones of the superiority of Western society and as members of the societies in question became aware of that, they objected to its use. A number of other terms are still in use: 'pre-industrial' and 'pre-literate' have also been objected to because of their overtones of 'backward'. 'Tribal' may be considered unacceptable for similar reasons, although in India and Bangladesh it is the official term for peoples who have never been incorporated into the caste hierarchy. 'Simple' and 'small-scale' have so far escaped serious criticism and 'non-industrial' avoids evolutionary implications. These three, together with the imprecise label 'traditional' are the most commonly used now.

All these terms are ways of designating the distinctive characteristics of the kinds of societies forming the bulk of anthropological studies. (Of course, as has been noted more than once, they are not the only societies social anthropologists are interested in.) Their chief distinguishing characteristic is that most people produce their own food and traditionally use no money. They are said to have a subsistence economy. This does not mean, as some people think, that they live close to a level of hunger or starvation, but that the economy is one of independence from outside; it provides subsistence. There is a difference between such societies and those in which people habitually exchange some of their produce for other goods, while aiming to be self-sufficient in food. The second kind are often called peasant societies to distinguish them. They are connected, both politically and economically, to centres which are the source of goods made by specialists, the sites of markets and often of government. The centres depend on the produce of peasants for their supply of food, although some may be grown in the vicinity.

It was once thought that the term 'economy' was not a suitable one to use where people do not have money and can therefore have no concept of price. Others have argued that this is a rather narrow definition of economics: they would define economics as the management of resources and their allocation to a variety of uses, which entails the exercise of choice. Using this broader approach, anthropologists like Raymond Firth have been able to use the concepts of economics to analyse the behaviour of subsistence farmers or fishermen and compare them with Western 'economic man'. They have shown that, far from being traditionalists who doggedly follow customary practices, such people calculate, plan ahead and adopt new practices. They do so just as easily (or with just as much reluctance) as people involved in a money economy who buy their food from commercial farmers. These insights should be of importance to development experts, who are inclined to blame the failure of their plans on a reluctance to change traditional ways, the 'dead weight of custom'.

Such contributions from anthropologists have attracted the attention of some economists; they have stimulated debate about the nature of an economy and the degree to which it can be analysed apart from social values and the society of which it is a part. In non-industrial economies, there are no specialized economic institutions like banks and firms. The economic system is an aspect of social organization, so those who are particularly interested in analysing it must consider the economic implications of a wide variety of social arrangements. The ceremonial presentation of gifts can be a means of distributing goods, utilizing the services of specialists and stimulating the production of surplus food, as well as cementing social relations, establishing peace or marking a ritual occasion. However, gift-giving in industrialized societies is by no means insignificant, as one anthropologist discovered. In 1972 the gift industry accounted for 120,000 jobs and 1.8 per cent of all manufacturing sales; consumers spent half what they spend on clothes on gifts, accounting for over four per cent of all consumer expenditure. The value of manufacturing sales of gifts was greater than the value of sales in the shipbuilding and marine engineering industry, and approached the value of total sales from coal mining. Clearly, the use of gifts to express and strengthen relationships does not cease when there are specialized economic institutions to organize production and distribution, indicating perhaps that market economies are less independent of society than has been assumed.

The exchange of ideas between economists and anthropologists is still limited to rather a few specialists on each side, who have acquired enough expertise in the other subject to engage in technical debates. But all social anthropologists doing field-work are expected to find out what use the people they study make of the sources of food they choose from the environmental possibilities that are available. This entails understanding the social values according to which these choices are made, and the effect of restrictions they may entail. There are no peoples who eat everything that is edible; there are always some things that a culture defines as inedible. We do not eat dogs, but dog-meat may be a delicacy in other parts of the world. A calendar of seasonal activities is a necessary background to the description of social events, which may require the collection of extra amounts of food and the mobilization of more labour than usual. In fact, the distribution of tasks and the organization of work is an important aspect of many social relations; the obligation of relatives to help one another may have major economic implications where there is no concept of paid labour. The ability to marry more than one wife may have quite different connotations in one society where women do most of the agricultural tasks than in another where wives are an economic liability. Indeed, for anthropologists who use a Marxist approach, understanding the economy is fundamental, for they believe that it ultimately determines the form of the social system. Not all social anthropologists share this assumption, but most would agree that a consideration of the material aspects of social life must be included in any analysis.

A consideration of the economy will include finding out how goods are distributed, whether some people have more of them than others and what they do with their wealth. In simple societies, the absence of money or other goods which might act as a store of wealth encourages the distribution of surplus goods. Wealth often consists, not of living in a different style from others who are poorer, but in supporting large numbers of dependents, or being able to call on the services of people whom you have helped with gifts. Wealth of this sort confers power; it may or may not be a source of prestige and the admiration of others. Power and prestige are important elements in any political system so that the political and economic aspects of society are closely linked.

There are two sides to the description and analysis of a political system: positions of authority and the institutions which maintain law and order on the one hand, and competition for power on the other. In the early years of this century political scientists tended to confine themselves to the study of specialized institutions such as the state, parliaments, courts, kings, judges and their agents, such as the police. Hereditary rulers, the chiefs and kings of Asia and Africa were considered more or less primitive prototypes of more 'advanced' political systems. Some societies, however, like the cattle-keeping Nuer, seemed to have no leaders at all, let alone rulers. In such places it was assumed that everyone followed custom so slavishly that there was no need of government. Unless there were governmental institutions that were recognizably similar to those of Europe, they argued, one could not talk of government. In publishng a group of studies of African political systems some anthropologists challenged this view. They argued that in all societies there is a mechanism whereby order is maintained, and by which people can be mobilized by authorities, authorities who may not be recognized as political officials but are effective leaders. These scholars placed rather more emphasis on the framework of the political system, the means by which boundaries were marked out and leaders emerged, the powers of rulers and the ritual basis of their authority, than is currently the case. Today it is necessary also consider informal politics; not merely the chief's position but if individuals compete for the position, how they do so; the connection between the right to rule and the power to enforce decisions. Others have studied nationalist parties and their predecessors under colonialism, or the politics of ethnic groups in mixed societies. There is a shift towards studying the distribution of power in society, not merely the institutions of government.

In all societies there are certain individuals who break the rules; conflicts occur, disputes must be settled. The ways in which this is done may vary quite widely, from public stoning at one end of the spectrum, to general ostracism of an offender at the other. It is quite untrue to say that simple societies are more peaceful and do not need police and prisons because there are no offenders; or that it was contact with Western ways that has introduced conflict among them. In all societies most people are kept in line because they do not wish to incur the penalties they expect will follow. Malinowski's great contribution to our understanding of this process was to demonstrate the great importance of the obvious fact that we are all social beings, who depend on the cooperation of others. In a small society where each individual depends on the help of others in all sorts of situations, the enmity of other people, their gossip or refusal to lend a hand when asked, may be a powerful way of bringing people into line. Even in England, the reminder 'You will make Daddy angry', 'What will your aunt think?', or 'What will the neighbours say?' may be used to warn people. Anthropological studies have shown how the fear of witchcraft makes for conformity to a code of behaviour, either in case one is accused of being a witch, or because the people one has injured may bewitch you in revenge. In studying any society, the field-worker must be aware of the multiple pressures that may be exerted, both to prevent disputes and also to make people settle their differences when conflict does break out. If one defines law as the institutions which administer it, then many societies have no law; however, all societies have law in the sense that they do not live in anarchy. Where this is so, the settlement of disputes and the maintenance of accepted rights and duties is an aspect of the total system, in the same way that the political and economic systems are embedded in more general relationships. One can see that anthropology has proceeded in the same way in all three cases. Reacting against the specialists on these subjects, who define their subject of study in accordance with what they know of their own society and ones like it, anthropologists have said, in effect: 'All right, if simple societies have no money, governmental institutions or courts, what does an economic (or political or legal) system do? Can we find other institutions which perform the same function in simple societies?' This word 'function', has become an important technical term in anthropology, so it is as well to consider it in more detail.

***The concept of function***   In the sense that it is used above, 'function' merely indicates that some aspect of social life serves some social purpose. It is useful. Not that the people concerned may recognized this; indeed, they probably do not. So one cannot say that the people have designed it to be like that. If threats of witchcraft act as a form of social control, this is not to say that people who are afraid of witches know this. This way of looking at social institutions replaced the unsatisfactory explanations of the evolutionists. A particular custom was not just meaningless tradition, it contributed to society as a whole. Some writers used the analogy with a living being, arguing that, just as organs of the body are necessary for it to exist, so social institutions contribute to the maintenance of a society. This analogy is not particularly helpful, in that it implies that particular social institutions or usages may be good for society, or even that without them society would not survive. But a society is not like a living organism, it does not die. Individuals die, but unless a whole population is wiped out (and this has happened), a society will continue in some form, even if it changes. Moreover the term 'function' is imprecise in other ways; it has been used by some to imply the *effects* of a particular social feature and by others to mean its *cause*. The slipperiness of the word has allowed some social anthropologists to confuse *purpose* (what the people see as a reason for doing something) and *effects* (what the observer understands as its contribution to the whole). Indeed, 'function' came to have so many meanings that it outlived its usefulness, which was to emphasize the interconnectedness of all aspects of social life. But, as Lucy Mair has pointed out (see her book listed in Appendix A) the attitude of mind which produced this concept has changed much less. Social anthropologists continue to be interested in how a social system works, and to see the particular aspect they are studying as part of a whole. The essential task is to relate ideas and behaviour to the total context, exploring all possible connections with other aspects of society. To do this effectively one must observe at first hand what actually goes on, so that the concept of function is closely linked to the emphasis on field-work.

***Kinship and the concept of social structure*** An important part of any field study concerns the kinship system of the people concerned. By this term social anthropologists mean all relationships organized by the idea of common ancestry, including also relationships established by marriage. Kinship is commonly thought to be relatively unimportant in industrial societies, being largely a matter of marriage and the family. This may not be entirely accurate, but there is no doubt that kinship is a very important part of the social organization of any non-industrial society; in some of them it provides the main structure of the society. There are a number of different aspects, for example, the system of naming – but how relatives are classified is an area in which the difference from Western society is very marked. English, for example, distinguishes what we call 'family members' from relatives outside the family; this is not so in most of the world. For example, there may be one term for a whole range of male kin, including the man who would be referred to as 'father' in English. Putting it in this rather clumsy way shows up the difficult problem of translation that this sort of difference entails. If we translate the term as 'father', we are implying that the other men who are also addressed as father are somehow not 'real' fathers, that the name is used for them as a sort of metaphor or out of courtesy. Alternatively, one can assume, as early social anthropologists did, that such people really do not know who their 'real' father is. Field research has shown that in fact people do make distinctions within a set of kin called by the same term, but it is also true that relatives called by a single term (like cousin in English) are considered as very much the same. The comparative study of such naming systems, or kinship terminologies, some of which are very complex, has become highly specialized, but kinship relations are so important in simple societies that no field-worker can afford to ignore kinship altogether.

Kinship determines much of the everyday behaviour of people in small-scale societies. The terms that people use in speaking to one another imply the sort of behaviour that is appropriate. Some kin must maintain formal behaviour with one another, while others are allowed more freedom and licence. In particular, some kin are marriageable and some are not; still others may be considered ideal spouses. The variation in these systems indicates just how little our ideas of relatedness have to do with the facts of reproduction; these relationships are socially determined. However, the problem of deciding just what is the relationship between the social definition of relatedness and other factors, such as similarities with other social animals, is a matter of debate between socio-biologists or animal behaviourists and social anthropologists. The determination of what, if any, are the universals in kinship systems is also a matter of discussion.

The wide significance of kinship in many simple societies is because it is multi-purpose. Kinship relations may have importance in many different fields of social activity. In societies where one cannot acquire the means of producing one's livelihood, or mobilize labour for any enterprise, except through relatives, kinship is bound to be vital. By contrast, where productive resources can be bought and labour hired, kinship may lose its significance in these areas, although it may still be important in providing a safety net in times of trouble. The quality that distinguishes kinship from other kinds of relationship is that it is both fixed (one cannot choose who one is related to) and it is supported by the deepest moral convictions. Kinship systems in non-industrial societies include a far wider range of people under this rubric, with the result that in many communities all relationships are kinship ones. Indeed, in some small societies if a stranger cannot establish kinship links with his host community, he may be considered an enemy, and be attacked.

In many societies, the most important social groups are based on descent from a common ancestor. These groups may own rights to important resources, may organize religious activities or may form the basis of all political action. In some cases they perform all three functions. They also vary in form and significance, and the comparative study of descent in differing social systems is an important field of enquiry. The manner in which such groups are defined, their internal structure and the way in which they are integrated into society as a whole, has been the subject of fierce controversies: between those who emphasize their kinship basis, and others who claim that descent groups are determined by the way they are bound together in systems of marriage alliance.

The field of kinship, in which social anthropologists are the sole experts, is the traditional heartland of social anthropology. It also exemplifies rather well what is meant by social structure, since in the classic cases, such as the aboriginal societies of Australia, kinship *is* the social structure. In general, structure refers to the ordering of parts to form a whole. The parts of a social structure are social groups, relationships and roles. The last term refers to the part played by someone in a particular position, such as mother, teacher, or bus-conductor. The position is socially defined, that is, the right and duties pertaining to it, the pattern of behaviour expected, are common to all who occupy it, while each individual will also play the role in a distinctive manner. Individual variations reflect personality, but also the fact that each living person plays a number of different roles, involving different sets of people, and the roles may affect one another. A professor will play her role of mother differently from a part-time nurse.

Looked at from this angle, a kinship system is also a series of roles defined in relation to one another. The role of mother implies children, that of aunt, nephews and nieces; roles imply relationships. The totality of relationships of different kinds constitutes the structure of society. In some societies there are no relationships which are not defined by kinship, as in the case I cited, where not to be a kinsman is to be without any position except that of enemy. In other societies roles may be defined as elements in political, economic or other institutions; the relationship of each set of roles to the total structure must be worked out in each case.

In any small community, everyone knows how they are related or assume they are 'cousins' or some general category of kin; the anthropologist, as a stranger, has to find this out.

Much of the essential work in the first few months of field-work is spent in discovering what this background of general knowledge consists of. Often quarrels and friendships only become intelligible when one knows how the people involved are related. It is an investigation which quickly shows up the assumptions that we all have about how people should behave. For example, in British society brothers and sisters are expected to be on terms of informality, though they may not see very much of one other when they grow up. In many other societies, such as the Trobriands for example, adult brothers and sisters are on extremely formal terms, avoiding each other's company, and never presuming to mention subjects of conversation which would be appropriate for people on terms of intimacy. In each case the people concerned think the behaviour of brothers and sisters is 'natural', spontaneous and explained only by itself. They say that brothers and sisters behave that way because they are brothers and sisters; the social anthropologist, comparing the two societies realizes that such behaviour is taught, not natural at all. If it were natural, it would be the same in all societies. One of the firmest conclusions of social anthropology is that people assume that their own behaviour is 'natural' and that of others odd. Human behaviour is not endlessly plastic, but it can vary between very wide limits. So field-work itself becomes an exercise in comparative understanding, by confronting one with how different people can be. It also makes clear why field-work in societies which resemble one's own is so difficult; there is no automatic contrast to alert one to what might otherwise be taken for granted as 'natural behaviour'. By their acts and ideas the people being studied show the anthropologist his or her own culturally specific notions.

*Ethnocentricity*   In studying human society, the greatest handicap is that we are, ourselves, products of a particular society. All human beings see the world through the ideas and concepts which they have acquired in the society they have grown up in. We, like everyone else, consider that we are seeing the world as it is. We feel that people who see things differently are ignorant, or prejudiced, or both. This attitude is referred to as ethnocentricity. A fascinating example of it, which provoked heated arguments among well-known anthropologists, is the question of how different people understand 'the facts of life'. There are some famous cases where it has been reported that people believe that the cause of conception is not sexual intercourse, but the entry of a spirit into the woman concerned. The anthropologists' debate centred on how this belief was to be interpreted, since the observation of domestic animals seemed to have produced an understanding of reproduction, which we would think is more in accord with 'the facts'. An American anthropologist contributing to the discussion, reported a conversation he had had on Yap island with a number of islanders. They were quite prepared to agree that the reason they had imported European boars was to improve the quality of their pigs by cross-breeding the boars with native sows. Yet they refused to accept the idea that sexual relations among humans resulted in pregnancy, citing various cases of married women without children, and ugly women, whom no one found attractive, having babies. The discussion produced puzzlement on both sides, until light dawned on a particularly intelligent islander: 'Ah', he said to his companions, 'this man actually believes that people are the same as pigs'. To put this finally in perspective, another anthropologist has recently shown that our ideas of facts of life, which support relations between parents and children, are not as firmly based on scientific knowledge as we fondly imagine. They were held firmly long before science was able to demonstrate what the process of reproduction entailed. The end product of the whole debate was not only a greater understanding of the ideas of other people, but also the clarification of the relationship between such ideas and kinship relations in our own society as well.

*Marriage as a 'social concept'* The contribution social anthropology can make to an understanding of society in general, including the one we live in, is very well demonstrated by examples from yet another aspect of kinship which is probably more important in other parts of the world: marriage. In Western society marriage is primarily thought of in two contexts, the founding of a family and romantic love. These ideas are significant parts of our culture but they have proved to be unhelpful as concepts to use in comparative analysis. The idea of romantic love may exist in other societies, although it is rarely as highly developed as it is in Western social life, but it may be quite unconnected with marriage. If we consider the social relationships involved, it becomes clear that marriage involves the linking of two sets of relations, often two separate groups, in an alliance. Often these alliances are arranged by senior kin and accompanied by gifts either exchanged, or given by one side to the other, as a further cementing of the new relationship. The ceremonies, which mark its beginning, involve kin on both sides; an important part of any study of marriage is a detailed analysis of who is involved on both sides, and what their commitment entails.

A possible conclusion from this is that marriage is quite different in the West from marriage in other societies; but this is only partly true. Weddings in industrialized societies are better understood once it is recognized that they too represent the establishment of new connections between sets of people. This is represented formally in the church with the aisle dividing the 'sides', and later in the mixed group reception. Moreover, although we believe that the choice of a marriage partner is a most individual matter, the influence of social factors has been most amply demonstrated by studying who people actually choose to marry. Their choices can be shown to follow a pattern in much the same way as in arranged marriages; in Western marriages bride and groom are usually from similar backgrounds and communities, with similar interests. Their 'free' choice is influenced by their ideas of what marriage entails, the class and regional structure of their society.

This example can help to clarify the formal distinction made in the last chapter, between people and society. Any wedding is the result of decisions made by people, their particular circumstances, individual personalities and private feelings; it also displays a social pattern which is repeated with minor variations in each wedding, since the ideas about what marriage should be, or usually is, and the social pressures to conform are common to all. The view which the participants have of their actions is not the same as that of the social anthropologist observing them; and though the latter must use each wedding as a means of finding out what weddings are in any society, it is the social, not the individual elements that anthropology is interested in.

In industrialized societies marriage is so often linked with the family as though they were two sides of a coin, that one anthropologist wished to call a book she was writing 'Marriage, and not the Family' to make her subject matter clear. In most societies marriage is expected to result in children, and some peoples do not consider the marriage itself as complete until children are born. However, the term 'family' also implies setting up house together, and may confuse several distinct elements which social anthropologists keep separate. The question of where newly-married couples live must be discovered by research, and there are a great variety of such arrangements, including ones where husband and wife do not share the same house at all. Even where they do they are always linked by ties of kinship with other households, so the idea of an isolated domestic group as the building block of society is inaccurate. It is often not at all easy to decide what the pattern is in a particular society; the significance of marriage is one element which affects the picture but there are many others: the allocation of work, rights to different resources, obligations to feed people, or to work for them. All these must be considered in relation to the central question of the place of husband, wife and children in the kinship system and in residential arrangements.

In the course of building up a body of ideas on this subject, some anthropologists as well as sociologists have come to the conclusion that the term 'family' is too ethnocentric, too loaded with implications from a particular way of life, to use as a technical term. The social sciences have a particular problem in this respect. Since all languages contain terms which refer to aspects of social life, it seems at first sight as though one need not construct a separate technical vocabulary in order to discuss society. Terms in common use, however, have a particular social loading and are often imprecise, with many shades of meaning. Some social scientists have preferred to coin new terms, in order to indicate precisely what they mean; but the development of jargon often results in writing which is incomprehensible, except to specialists, and sometimes not even to them. Others still use ordinary language but define words in a particular way, trying to make them more neutral. A concern with definitions is particularly characteristic of social anthropological writing, since the work itself makes those who engage in it more than usually conscious of the ethnocentricity of their language. Students often complain of what they see as pedantic discussions about words; but the attempt to be objective about society and to compare social forms requires them to be aware of the meanings of words such as 'the family', in order not to build into their work terms which are loaded with ethnocentric connotations.

***Religion and concept of culture***   So far this chapter has covered most of the central area of social anthropology. In discussing the economic, political, legal and kinship systems, two concepts – structure and function – have been sufficient to allow the reader to obtain some idea of the subject matter of research and discussion. In order to complete the discussion, a new concept is required. This is 'culture' in its technical meaning, which has changed considerably over time and has rather different meanings in Britain and in the United States, where cultural anthropology is more widely taught than social anthropology. It is also rather different in approach. A full discussion of the term will also need some reference to the work of French anthropologists, notably Lévi-Strauss, whose work has been very influential in the last few decades.

The reason that we can proceed no further without the concept of culture is that the comparative study of religion, within social anthropology, is centrally concerned with symbolism, and the way in which social ideas and relationships are represented. The social anthropological study of religion starts from the assumption that one is not concerned with the 'truth' or 'falsehood' of a religion. Instead, the anthropologist is interested in how religious activities are organized, and how they mobilize people in common action, the position and powers of religious specialists of various kinds, and the common beliefs and practices of a society which define the world for them: the cosmology. Christianity can be studied in the same ways as ancestral cults; the effect of witchcraft beliefs can be examined without having to consider whether witches actually exist. The problem of defining religion in such a way that the term can be used for comparison is long-standing, and there are various definitions which attempt to deal with the ethnocentric assumptions which the word tends to have. It is not necessary to go into it here, merely to point out that religion has been studied, either through its actions and the groups and relationships involved in them, or through beliefs. Until comparatively recently social anthropology favoured the first approach which allowed the focus on social structure which was central to their work. The emphasis on belief tended to ignore the ritual activities, which are part of a religion, in favour of more or less sophisticated interpretations of how a set of beliefs in spiritual beings or powers came about.

*Culture* The concentration on religious action – ritual – eventually posed questions of interpretation that indicated that both these approaches were unable to deal with social variations of a particular sort; societies have distinctive forms of ritual behaviour, which are not adequately explained by noting what social relationships they represent. The objects used in ritual, the songs, prayers and dances represent a wealth of meanings which are relevant in secular life as well. To take an example: in many African societies, a sacrifice to the ancestors of a descent group brings together all its members. In addition, children of members of the descent group who have married out of it and who are not members themselves may attend, as well as spouses of members. The people who officiate at the ritual are the senior members of the group so that the whole ritual shows clearly the descent group and its connections, through kinship and marriage, with other similar groups. The beliefs which are associated with the activity and explain it to the participants are beliefs in ancestral spirits and their powers. This sketch shows that one can discuss an ancestral sacrifice without considering what the ritual actually consists of: whether people kill an animal, and what kind this is, the meaning of the words used, or the way in which a blessing is conveyed. A large part of the ritual is left unexplained and some crucial differences between societies may be ignored. This aspect concerns symbolism which, like much that is social, contains broad themes which are found in many places, together with specific forms that characterize particular societies. In striving for a different approach which would allow them to include symbolism in their analysis, social anthropology has revived the term 'culture', which had lapsed from the technical vocabulary for various reasons, although it remained in use in the United States.

The original nineteenth-century definition of culture, which was accepted as precise enough for technical usage, was 'that complex whole, which includes knowledge, belief, art, morals, law, custom and any other capabilities and habits acquired by man as a member of society'. It was essentially a comprehensive list of what members of a society have in common and has been summarized as 'learned behaviour'. It covers much the same ground as the concept of society but with a different emphasis: on a body of custom which is taught and handed down from generation to generation, rather like a tool-kit for living. It does not distinguish between the trivial and the significant, between table-manners and political rules, techniques (or the art) of hunting and the organization of descent groups.

In developing this concept, British anthropologists used the notion of institutions to order items of culture according to their significance. Subsequently, the concept of structure, of social relations and roles placed the emphasis on morals, law and custom but reorganized the material in accordance with the new ideas. In the United States, culture has remained the basic concept, except among those who were trained in Britain or who have made a special study of social anthropology. Cultural anthropology has retained much closer links with both physical anthropology and archaeology than social anthropology, for the concept of culture was formulated when these subjects were barely distinguished from one another. It clearly facilitates a common approach.

In Britain, by contrast, the study of material culture has developed part of the content of the original definition of culture into a separate study. The term 'art' stood for 'skills' and included not only aesthetic skills, like carving or music, but weaving, iron work and basic food-getting techniques. Material culture studies all these aspects of learned behaviour, their distribution and changes over time. It has become more distant from social anthropology as the latter dropped the term culture from its repertoire of concepts.

In modern British usage, culture refers to a rather narrower range of items than the original definition covered: it is concerned with knowledge, and belief – in the sense of ideas about the world as well as religious belief. It includes social concepts and meaning, and could be better glossed as modes of thought. One may include under that label meaning which is implicit, or conveyed in myth, and ways of understanding the world which are not clearly spelled out, but are underlying assumptions. The term culture brings together the study of symbolism in ritual and in secular life, knowledge and systems of classification of plants and animals, traditional medicine and divination and a range of esoteric bodies of learning, which are the province of specialists like shamans (spirit mediums), artists and dancers. Although much of the study of folk knowledge and classification is now a specialization within anthropology, the study of social relations has been enriched by this new approach which allows for a greater appreciation of social variety without sacrificing the benefits of the study of society's structure.

In France, the famous anthropologist, Lévi-Strauss developed a method of structural analysis which should not be confused with the British concept of social structure. His underlying assumptions derive from the work of the American, Boas, and the school of cultural anthropology as it was then. He has used a method devised in linguistics for the analysis of phonemics to study myth, specifically the myths of South American Indians. He has also applied the technique to the study of kinship and totemism. His major work *Mythologiques*, is probably the *Golden Bough* of the twentieth century, and aims, through an encyclopaedic study of detail, to understand the structure of thought. His work has influenced social anthropology in both Britain and France. To my mind, it has had less lasting influence in Britain for a number of reasons. Culture as a basic rather than a supplementary concept displays a number of weaknesses; it tends to remain at the level of ideas. The approach to the study of society through the concepts of social structure and social relations, allows one to deal with the interplay between ideas and action, ideals of behaviour and what people actually do, in a manner which permits an understanding of the observed reality of other people's lives.

*Modern developments*   Social anthropology in Britain has burgeoned since the end of the Second World War. New departments have been set up and the numbers of anthropologists have grown by leaps and bounds; an enormous corpus of knowledge has been amassed. Some people have argued that it is now in danger of splitting into several different fields of study, along lines that have been indicated from time to time. This account has had to ignore many of the recent developments in order to present a simplified general account. It would have been foolish to try and cover all the various theoretical developments of recent years in the space of a few pages; most of them originate in the subject as it is depicted here, which still represents the core of most university courses in the subject.

In France and the United States there are also a number of schools of thought; in France, Marxist anthropology and the old-fashioned intensive ethnography form two sides of a triangle, of which the third is the school of Lévi-Strauss. In the United States the effect of these developments in Europe has also made itself felt; British social anthropology is also much admired and becoming more influential, although in a recognizably American form. In discussing basic concepts, I have been concerned to indicate broad differences, rather than details of theoretical divergences. Readers should be aware, however, that American text-books on cultural anthropology are no introduction to the subject as it is taught in Britain and may prove confusing. Similarly, the works of Lévi-Strauss are not a guide to social anthropology, however fascinating in themselves they may be.

Social anthropology is a subject for those with an independent mind. This does not mean merely those who question present social arrangements, for critics of society can be just as rigidly ethnocentric as conformists. It is not for those who do not wish to examine their own assumptions nor for those who hope for guidance in a difficult world. It provides endless fascination for those who enjoy analysing a problem into its constituent elements, who relish the challenge of finding the best interpretation for a set of facts, setting one authority beside another and making up their minds about which to accept. Perhaps the most interesting thing about the subject is that it attracts a variety of individualists, who are often argumentative but never dull.

# 3

## The uses of Social Anthropology

The question 'What use is a degree in Social Anthropology?' often expresses the residual doubts of a parent, teacher or a prospective student, about whether it is worth investing the three years of a university course in a subject which is new and relatively unknown. Law, Medicine and Accountancy, for example, are known to lead directly to professional qualifications; Classics, English or History are believed to train the mind in various ways, although not, in themselves, preparing one for a particular career. The relevance of the knowledge conferred by a degree in Economics or Politics to a number of jobs is easy to see. To most people, the unfamiliarity of social anthropology makes it difficult to assess in any of these ways. But it combines a rigorous intellectual training of a stimulating kind with knowledge that can be put to good use in many different posts. More and more, this is being recognized by employers; even those who know little about the subject are coming to accept a degree in Social Anthropology as being like any non-professional university training: it is not sufficient in itself to guarantee the holder a job, but it is an excellent general education.

Of course, the best reason for studying social anthropology, or any other subject for that matter, is that it is absorbingly interesting. Unless students are really interested in their subject, they will find work tedious, will not do as well as they could do, and may even conclude that university life is disappointing. So it is important to be reasonably sure about the course. Because hardly any schools teach social anthropology, some people opt to read it at university just because it is unknown. It seems exciting as it is unlike anything they have studied so far. This is not a good reason for doing it. Social anthropology requircs intellectual effort from the beginning, for the simple reason that it cannot rely on basic principles having been acquired at school and must cover a lot of ground in three or four years. If after reading this book there are still doubts, then the reading list at the end of the book provides examples of anthropological writing to give the flavour of work in the first year. It should deter only those who have chosen social anthropology because it looks different and not because it looks interesting.

## Aptitude and exams

Even if students are thoroughly convinced that they want to study social anthropology, a second question is often raised: 'What "O" or "A" levels are best in this situation?' Sometimes it is not clear what is meant by this question; it might mean 'What "A" ("O") levels will members of a department of social anthropology prefer when they are assessing candidates for places?' or 'What best indicates intellectual qualities that will find the degree course interesting?' or even 'How can someone prepare for a course in social anthropology?' Sometimes the questioner is not really sure which of these questions is important. To be clear it is best to answer them separately.

To start with the first question, there are no 'O' or 'A' levels which someone *must* have to read the subject. Assessors look for good spread of 'O' levels, indicating a general education; they would probably question the application if there were few 'O' levels and those taken included no maths as this gives some indication of an analytical mind. Those universities who still require certain 'O' level subjects do not make exceptions for new subjects. In general, however, 'O' level subjects are only important as a general guide to the sort of education an applicant has had and what level he or she reached. Poor 'O' levels can, of course, be wiped out by good 'A' levels. None of them particularly qualify a student, although someone intending to include physical anthropology in the degree course will find it a help to know some biology and genetics beforehand.

Social anthropologists expect to start teaching their subject from scratch and often prefer to do so; an 'A' level in sociology, economics or government is no particular advantage. A range of 'A' levels which indicate artistic talents or an ability to learn languages may indicate someone whose bent is *not* suited to social anthropology, unless there is also evidence of ability to analyse, formulate an argument and criticize ideas as well. Some social anthropology teachers consider history a good guide, but people who have an 'A' level background in science subjects may be accepted and indeed do very well.

The best preparation for the subject is to be clear what it involves and to have read something about it. An indication that social anthropology might suit a particular student may lie in their inability to decide between arts and sciences, so that 'O' level and 'A' level choices are rather mixed. Many schools include some exposure to social sciences, even if they do not teach them for examination purposes; an interest in the social sciences generally and in the range of topics they cover, is a good indication that social anthropology might interest a student. A point that should perhaps be made is that an interest in exotic places is not enough.

## Social anthropology and careers

A degree course in Social Anthropology imparts skills which are shared with other disciplines, but has its own particular approach which is distinctive. Students learn to reason accurately and express an argument on paper in essays, they discuss the strengths and weaknesses of particular theories in seminars. It is characteristic of social anthropology that it constantly relates ideas to 'facts'. As it is firmly based in empirical research, theories are evaluated against data, but information gathering must include analysis. For example, a student may be asked to write an essay on witchcraft among the Azande of the Sudan; the finished essay will be expected to discuss the ideas of Evans-Pritchard, the main source for this topic, together with those of his critics and others who have studied witchcraft elsewhere. What is being taught is not merely how to understand the Azande but how to analyse witchcraft in a comparative framework and relate the analysis to a body of ideas. Students will be expected to understand figures as well: tables of frequencies may be as important as beliefs and 'customs' for the understanding of some aspect of social life such as household structure or patterns of marriage. The teaching of social anthropology relies less on standard texts than many other courses, which forces its students to search out relevant material, make their own comparisons and draw their own conclusions, thus developing an experience which can form a good basis for any sort of independent work.

Such skills are widely relevant to jobs in the Civil Service, local government, journalism, radio and television, market research and information services; in fact, any career which requires a mind trained to collect, assess and communicate information. The skills are not unique to social anthropology but have been stressed in order to show that social anthropology is not just a matter of 'learning about other societies' but a training in how social anthropologists think and analyse information in order to reach their conclusions. While graduate work is a more specific training in methods of research and involves personal experience of field-work, an undergraduate is expected to develop some skills of the same kind.

The distinctive approach of social anthropology lies in two features: the fact that it is concerned with the interrelation of institutions within society and the attempt to eliminate ethnocentricity. Learning to perceive the interconnections between religious, political, economic and other institutions alerts the mind to the unintended consequences of actions or policies, the possibility of effects outside the area immediately concerned. The behaviour of consumers – of a product, patients in a clinic, or the clients of a social service – is produced by the interaction of many factors of their social life, not just the immediate situation, and social anthropology graduates are trained to consider this. The pursuit of objective understanding is an important means of liberating the mind to think creatively, to innovate and explore avenues which others might not perceive. Since even social anthropologists are members of particular societies, all social determination of thought cannot be eliminated, but social anthropology does force people to examine their own assumptions about how society is, or should be, organized. A recognition of the fact that ways of thinking and acting, perceiving problems or understanding the world are neither divinely ordained nor natural, but variable, is an important step in making one less prone to prejudging all sorts of issues. Some anthropologists feel strongly that social anthropology should be taught in all schools, not because children in them come from different cultures, but in order to eliminate prejudice itself. While opinions differ as to the effectiveness of such a measure, there is no doubt that the attitude of mind engendered by social anthropology is useful in any large-scale society with many different sub-cultures.

The specialized knowledge acquired during a degree course in Social Anthropology can find a number of uses. There are posts which require knowledge about particular parts of the world or particular peoples but these are often more suitable for graduates with research experience. However, museums and any post involving work abroad will find the ability to gather information and use it to understand local political events and parties, social attitudes and beliefs of all kinds a considerable asset. Such work includes the diplomatic service, posts with international firms or the British Council and research agencies of many kinds, as well as relief and development work for United Nations or charitable organizations.

The role of social anthropology in relief and development work deserves a particular mention. The human factor in social or material development, and in the relief of disasters, is the most important single element and too often it is either ignored or misunderstood. Over the last two decades or so, more and more examples of this have been accumulating. Many projects have had little or no success when they failed to take into account the people who would have to work them. Too often, for example, education in new crops and agricultural methods has been aimed at men in areas where it is women who do most of the farming. Some schemes have even had disastrous consequences for the very people they were intended to help. The Kainji dam on the Niger river was part of a development scheme designed to help the poor. But no account had been taken of the use made by local people of the annual flooding. When the dam controlled the floods, hundreds of thousands of people lost the chance to fish in the flood waters and fishing production was halved. Yam and rice production also declined without the fertilizing alluvium of the floods and there was no longer any dry-season grazing for cattle. For very many people the dam was an unmitigated disaster.

The introduction of a cash-crop intended to raise the standard of living of a poor area has led, in more than one case, to a lowering of nutritional levels, particularly among women and children. In many areas the head of household, normally a man, is fed first and the food is produced on the household's land and only very rarely bought for cash, except in times of great scarcity. The introduction of cash-crops removed some land from food production so that less food was produced; the money obtained from selling the cash-crops was used by the head of household, who also continued to be fed first from a diminished stock of food, leaving women and children the losers.

Development agencies may spend time and resources on educational campaigns to alter practices which they consider harmful, but if they do not understand these practices the result is likely either to be a failure or the cause of other problems. Family planning programmes are a notorious area where little impact has been made. Even in China where success has been the result of state coercion, some of the unintended consequences of one- or two-child families are not very happy ones: late abortions, neglect of female babies and even, some authorities say, female infanticide, plus a growing population of the elderly who will soon have to be supported by a very much smaller number of able-bodied workers.

These are simple examples, but they can be matched with more complex ones. Large sums of money have been wasted in development without anything being achieved, for lack of understanding which could have been provided by anthropological expertise. This is slowly being recognized and the role of anthropologists in development and relief work is expanding. Often they may have to undergo additional training, but a basis in social anthropology increasingly has an advantage.

The utility of the social anthropological approach is not confined to planning and development in the so-called Third World. The body of ideas which constitute this expertise can be applied to industrial societies as well. An understanding of organizations derived from the study of traditional kingdoms, clan groups and small-scale political organizations involves general principles which can be applied in personnel management, industrial relations, management consultancy and administration at all levels. Social anthropologists have been employed to evaluate community housing projects in London, relations between doctors and patients in Wales, and the effects of unemployment. They may need to familiarize themselves with the methods of sociology or other disciplines to a larger extent, but these additional skills are easily acquired, since the basis for them may already be there. (See Appendix B). The social aspects of research in health care, in the social services and in problems such as alcoholism, adolescent delinquency or child abuse have involved social anthropologists in a wide variety of fields where their contribution is increasingly valued.

It would not surprise anyone to learn that social anthropologists have a role to play in all work in the field of race relations and the welfare of ethnic minorities. The reason is less because they have information about the beliefs and behaviour of such minorities, but more because they understand the role that cultural differences play in a community, and the very wide range of situations in which culturally-based assumptions may impede communication between people. An ability to probe for the reasons behind conflict and prejudice is ultimately of more value than merely acting as an interpreter for a particular minority, but social anthropologists are trained to do both. The ability to look at the majority in the same way as the minority, and to discount as far as possible the assumptions of their own group, is perhaps the most significant benefit that a degree in Social Anthropology has to offer.

In education, social anthropology has an expanding role. To teach at the university level a doctorate is essential. This entails field research undertaken as a graduate student attached to a university department, one of whose staff will supervise the work. The data collected are written up in the form of a thesis which must be acceptable to the examiners (usually two or three). The research of British students is supported by graduate awards from the Economic and Social Research Council, but there are not many of them and they are awarded to the most highly-qualified applicants. In recent years, the effect of cutbacks has been such that it is usually only those with a first-class degree, or one slightly lower in class but supported by a postgraduate degree like an MSc, who will get them. The openings for graduate work in social anthropology are few but the situation may not always be so gloomy. However, it would be only realistic for most people not to pin their hopes on a university career.

Job opportunities in the universities have also decreased following government action to force the universities to retrench. There are few posts advertised, although graduates with British doctorates do find posts abroad, in Australia, New Zealand and the United States or Canada. However, the demand for courses in social anthropology in colleges of further education, polytechnics and adult or continuing education has been growing. Many more such courses have been established and it is likely that some teaching posts will continue to be available. There are already a few 'A' level subjects which include some social anthropology in the syllabus, either as an optional component (Social Biology – Cambridge Board) or as material for comparison (Sociology – London Board). There is continued pressure for an 'A' level in social anthropology itself, and a number of CSE examinations on the subject have been introduced at various schools. It is often due to the energy of a teacher trained in social anthropology but largely responsible for teaching other subjects, that these advances have been made. Even where social anthropology is not taught for examination purposes, it is directly relevant to general studies courses, which often aim to teach pupils about the Third World, or are concerned to combat racial prejudice. The role of anti-racist or multi-cultural education, whether in schools or other training schemes, like that of the police, is a matter of continuing debate, but there is no doubt that social anthropologists can, and should, contribute significantly to it.

Social anthropology can be useful in such a variety of ways that one must take care not to seem to prescribe it as a universal panacea for the problems of modern society. As anyone trained in the subject should be aware, the formulation of policy and its administration involve more than clear thinking and innovative ideas. There are conflicting interests to be considered, as well as the availability and distribution of material resources and access to power. No single academic discipline can hope to provide solutions to the many problems, both within our own society and in the international community. Social anthropology provides a valuable perspective on all those problems which concern people, and an insight into ourselves which is unlike any other. Its contribution lies in training the mind to perceive connections between aspects of modern life, from an objective stance that is relatively free of the moral judgements which, as many people have noticed, generate heat rather than light.

# Appendix A: Further reading

All books are published in paperback except those marked with an asterisk.

**Introductions to the subject**
These are personal views of the subject, each author having a slightly different approach.
I.M. Lewis, *Social Anthropology in Perspective* (Penguin Books 1976).
E.R. Leach, *Social Anthropology* (Fontana Masterguides 1982).
L. Mair, *An Introduction to Social Anthropology* (Oxford University Press, second edn 1972).
D. Pocock, *Understanding Social Anthropology* (Teach Yourself Series, Hodder and Stoughton 1975). Includes exercises which form a good basis for group discussion.

**The history of anthropological ideas**
J.W. Burrow, *Evolution and Society: A Study in Victorian Social Theory* (Cambridge University Press 1966). The author is not a social anthropologist but a historian of ideas who has made a detailed study of the work of three of the subject's intellectual forbears.
E.E. Evans-Pritchard, *Social Anthropology* (Routledge 1951). A rather old-fashioned, general introduction but with a historical slant.
A. Kuper, *Anthropologists and Anthropology* (Cambridge University Press 1973). The development of British social anthropology in the twentieth century. The second (1983), revised edition is much more contentious than the first.

**Accounts of field-work**
Descriptions of what it is like to do field-work, rather than a discussion of methods.
E. Smith-Bowen (L. Bohannan), *Return to Laughter* (Harper and

Brothers, New York 1954). First published under a pseudonym, this is an amusing fictionalized account of the author's field-work with her husband among the Tiv of Nigeria in the early 1950s.

*A.F. Robertson, *Community of Strangers: A Journal of Discovery in Uganda* (Scolar Press 1978). A vivid account of field-work experiences in a mixed migrant community in Uganda between 1965 and 1966. Gives an excellent picture of the growth of under-standing as field-work progresses.

K.E. Read, *The High Valley* (Scribner 1965). Two years' field-work in a remote part of the highlands of eastern New Guinea (1954–56): more introspective than the other two but gives such accurate word pictures that one can imagine oneself there.

P. Loizos, *The Heart Grown Bitter: a Chronicle of Cypriot War Refugees* (Cambridge University Press 1981). Rather different from the others, since it is both a description of the author's field experiences and a sensitive account of what happened to those Greek Cypriots who became refugees from the Turks in 1974.

**Studies of particular topics and peoples (from first-year reading lists)**

B. Malinowski, *Argonauts of the Western Pacific* (Routledge 1932). A classic monograph, describing the ceremonial exchange which links a group of islands off New Guinea, and setting out in detail the ramifications into all aspects of social life in the Trobriand Islands.

L. Mair *Marriage* (Penguin Books 1971). A clear, comprehensive account of what anthropologists have to say about the institution.

J.W. Watson (ed.) *Between Two Cultures: Migrants and Minorities in Britain* (Blackwell 1977). A series of articles by social anthropologists, some of which appeared in the press.

J. Lee *The !Kung San: Men, Women and Work in a Foraging Society* (Cambridge University Press 1979). A study of the Bushmen of southern Africa, who have been exhaustively researched, mostly by Americans. This is rather a long book, and concentrates almost exclusively on the economic and ecological aspects of !Kung life, but is easy to read and interesting.

*J. Pitt-Rivers *The People of the Sierra* (Chicago University Press, first edn 1954). A study of an Andalusian village.

# Appendix B:  Degree courses in Social Anthropology

Social anthropology is taught within two rather different academic contexts. Most commonly the subject is located within the social sciences, with the courses including options or minority subjects in related disciplines such as linguistics, economics, politics, sociology, or with a language. In a smaller number of cases social anthropology is taught together with archaeology and physical anthropology (sometimes referred to as biological anthropology) as part of the study of humanity. The courses in social anthropology will not differ very much according to the context in which they are taught, although students will be encouraged to consider the relation between social anthropology and the other subjects with which it is taught, leading to slightly different emphases in each case. The list below is divided to show the distinction and students are advised to consider what additional interests they may have before making a choice: an interest in politics would best be catered for in the first kind of degree, an interest in archaeology would indicate the second.

Joint degrees, in which social anthropology is one component are more usual than single honours in just social anthropology. The title of the degree may indicate which is the major subject by putting it first; however, since it has not been possible to include details of courses here, these should be checked in the prospectuses of the universities concerned. In some universities, like the University of York, the Sociology Department includes some people who have been trained in social anthropology and whose teaching will probably reflect this, but unless a university advertises courses as courses in social anthropology, they have not been included. Nor does the list include those universities where social anthropology is listed as one of eight or nine components of a general course.

If you are interested in art in other societies or in special courses such as comparative medicine, women in society or development, you will find that single courses in these subjects may be listed in the prospectus. Queen's University, Belfast, is the only department to teach ethnomusicology (comparative music) and dance at present, but two or three departments teach the other subjects.

Polytechnics may teach some social anthropology. Oxford Polytechnic teaches a CNAA degree in Anthropology which is unusual but more is likely to be offered in the future. It is worth studying the prospectuses of the different polytechnics to find out what is available.

The Careers Research and Advisory Centre (CRAC) is a source of information on courses available. They publish a range of guides.

The CRAC *Degree Course Guides* give detailed comparisons of first degree courses in UK universities, polytechnics and colleges. They cover 34 individual subjects plus eight technological subjects grouped together.

CRAC *Graduate Studies* offers a comprehensive guide to postgraduate research and study facilities in the UK.

CRAC *Directory of Further Education* is the only guide to courses available at polytechnics and other institutions outside the university sector throughout the UK. It includes information on entry requirements, the standard of qualification to be obtained, the type of course and where it is available – giving full names, addresses and phone numbers of the institutions.

These guides are published by Hobsons, Ltd, Bateman Street, Cambridge CB2 1LZ and the information contained in them has been checked as carefully as possible. However, all institutions undergo changes in student numbers, staffing and research facilities and the courses on offer are thus subject to change. Intending students should ensure they consult the most recent editions, and get in touch with the institutions themselves before submitting applications.

The University Central Council on Admissions (UCCA) current *Handbook* should also be consulted.

Careers teachers at schools and the LEA Careers Guidance Officers should have these available for consultation. Many public libraries also keep copies and they are available through bookshops.

A more general book on student life and student institutions is published annually by Macmillan (Papermac), called *The Student Book*.

In order to set out the information as clearly as possible, the relevant addresses are listed separately after the degree list below.


**Social Anthropology as a social science**

*Single Honours*
*Belfast*: BA Honours Social Anthropology

*Edinburgh*: MA Honours (four year course) Social Anthropology

*Kent at Canterbury*: BA Single Honours Social Anthropology

*London* – London School of Economics: BA Honours Anthropology; BSc Honours with special subject Anthropology

*London* – School of Oriental and African Studies: BA Honours Social Anthropology

*Manchester*: BSocSc Honours Social Anthropology

*Sussex*: BA Honours Social Anthropology (in the School of African and Asian Studies)

*Swansea*: BA Single Honours Social Anthropology

### Joint Honours
(In the degree titles the sign '&' indicates two main subjects, 'with' shows that the subject that follows is a minor subject.)

#### Area Studies
South East Asian
*Kent*: BA Combined Honours Social Anthropology & South East Asian Studies

Burmese, Indonesian and Malay, Thai, Vietnamese
*London* – School of Oriental and African Studies: BA Two subject degrees Social Anthropology & an Area Study

Middle East
*St Andrews*: BA Honours Modern Middle Eastern Studies (not clear how much social anthropology)

American
*Swansea*: BA Joint degree Social Anthropology & American

#### Art History
*St Andrews*: MA Joint Honours Social Anthropology & Art History

#### Cognitive Studies
*Sussex*: BA Honours (in the School of Social Sciences) Social Anthropology with Cognitive Studies

#### Development Studies
*Kent*: BA Multi-disciplinary studies Development Studies & Social Anthropology

### Economics
*St Andrews*: MA Joint Honours Social Anthropology & Economics

*Stirling*: Joint BA Honours Economics & Social Anthropology

### Environmental Sciences
*Stirling*: BA Environmental Sciences & Social Anthropology

### Film & Media Studies
*Stirling*: Joint BA Honours Social Anthropology & Film and Media Studies

### Geography
*Durham*: BA Joint Honours Geography & Anthropology

*London*: University College BA or BSc Anthropology & Geography

*Manchester*: BA Honours Geography & Social Anthropology

*St Andrews*: MA Honours Geographical Studies with Social Anthropology; MA Joint Hons Social Anthropology & Geography

*Swansea*: BA Joint Honours Social Anthropology with Geography

### History
*Kent*: BA Interfaculty Honours History & Social Anthropology

*Manchester*: BA Honours History & Social Anthropology (provisional)

*Stirling*: Joint BA Honours History & Social Anthropology
Ancient History

*London* – University College: BA Honours Ancient History & Social Anthropology

Economic History
*Swansea*: BSc Econ. Economic History & Social Anthropology

Economic and Social History
*Belfast*: BA Joint Honours Economic and Social History & Social Anthropology

*St Andrews*: MA Joint Honours Social Anthropology & Economic and Social History

European History
*East Anglia*: BA Combined Honours (in the Schools of Modern Languages and European History) European History & Social Anthropology

Medieval History
*St Andrews*: MA Joint Honours Social Anthropology & Medieval History

Social History
*Swansea*: BSc Econ. Social Anthropology & Social History

### Linguistics
*Edinburgh*: MA Honours Social Anthropology & Linguistics

*London* – School of Oriental and African Studies: BA Joint Honours Social Anthropology & Linguistics

*London* – University College: BA Honours Anthropology & Linguistics

*Manchester*: BA Honours Linguistics & Social Anthropology

*Sussex*: BA Honours (in the School of Social Sciences) Social Anthropology with Linguistics

### Philosophy
*Belfast*: BA Joint Honours Philosophy & Social Anthropology; History & Philosophy of Science & Social Anthropology

*Kent*: BA Interfaculty Honours Philosophy & Social Anthropology

*St Andrews*: MA Honours Social Anthropology with Philosophy; MA Joint Honours Social Anthropology & Logic and Metaphysics; Social Anthropology & Moral Philosophy; Social Anthropology & Philosophy

*Swansea*: BA Joint Honours Social Anthropology with Philosophy

### Politics
*Belfast*: BA Joint Honours Politics & Social Anthropology

*Kent*: BA Combined Honours Social Anthropology & Politics and Government

*Stirling*: Joint BA Honours Politics & Social Anthropology

*Swansea*: BSc Econ. Politics & Social Anthropology

### Psychology
*Durham*: BA Joint Honours Anthropology & Psychology

*London* – Goldsmiths' College: BA Honours Social Anthropology & Psychology

*St Andrews*: MA Honours Social Anthropology with Psychology; MA Joint Honours Social Anthropology & Psychology

*Swansea*: BSc Econ. Psychology & Social Anthropology

### Social Psychology
*Kent*: BA Combined Honours Anthropology & Social Psychology

### Religious Studies
*London* – School of Oriental and African Studies: BA Joint Honours Social Anthropology & Religious Studies

### Sociology
*Aberdeen*: MA Sociology & Social Anthropology

*Belfast*: BA Joint Honours Social Anthropology & Sociology

*Durham*: BA Joint Honours Anthropology & Sociology

*Edinburgh*: MA Honours Social Anthropology & Sociology

*Hull*: BA Special degree Sociology & Social Anthropology

*Kent*: BA Combined Honours Anthropology & Sociology

*London* – Goldsmiths' College: BA Honours Anthropology & Sociology

*Salford*: BA Sociology with Social Anthropology

*Stirling*: Joint BA Honours Sociology & Social Anthropology

*Swansea*: BSc Econ. Social Anthropology & Sociology; BA Joint Honours Social Anthropology with Sociology

*Ulster*: BSc Honours (in the Faculty of Social and Health Sciences) Social Anthropology & Sociology

### Social Policy and Administration
*Kent*: BA Combined Honours Anthropology & Social Policy and Administration

### Social Statistics
*Kent*: BA Combined Honours Anthropology & Social Statistics

*Swansea*: BSc Econ. Social Anthropology & Social Statistics

**Combined Degrees**
(More than two subjects.)

*Cambridge*: BA Social and Political Sciences

*East Anglia*: BA Joint Honours (in the School of Economic & Social Studies) Politics and Sociology & Social Anthropology; Sociology & Social Anthropology and Economics; Sociology & Social Anthropology and Economics

*Salford*: BA/BSc Honours Social Science option includes Anthropology among the subjects offered

*Stirling*: BA combined Honours (Sociology, Social Administration and Social Anthropology)

*Ulster*: BSc Honours (in the Faculty of Social & Health Sciences) Social Anthropology & Sociology with Linguistics; Social Anthropology & Sociology with Philosophy; Combined Social Sciences

## Social Anthropology with Languages

*Danish, French, German, Norwegian, Swedish*
*East Anglia*: BA Combined Course (in the Schools of Modern Languages and European History) Social Anthropology & a language

*African (Hausa, Swahili), S. Asian (Bengali, Gujarati, Hindi, Marathi, Nepali, Oriya, Panjabi, Sinhalese, Tamil, Urdu)*
*London* – School of Oriental and African Studies: BA Joint Honours Social Anthropology & a language

*Spanish*
*St Andrews*: MA Honours Social Anthropology with Spanish; MA Joint Honours Social Anthropology & Spanish

*Stirling*: Joint BA Honours Social Anthropology & Spanish

## Social Anthropology in the field of the Human Sciences

*Single Honours*
*Cambridge*: BA Archaeology and Anthropology (students specialize after first year)

*Durham*: BA Honours Anthropology

*London* – University College: BA Honours Anthropology

*Oxford*: BA Human Sciences (Social and Physical Anthropology)

**Joint Honours**
*Belfast*: BA Honours Archaeology & Social Anthropology

*Durham*: BSc Joint Honours Archaeology & Anthropology; Anthropology & Zoology

*Edinburgh*: MA Honours Archaeology & Social Anthropology

**Addresses of universities where Anthropology is taught**
*Aberdeen*: University of Aberdeen, Aberdeen AB9 1FX

*Belfast*: The Queen's University, University Road, Belfast BT7 1NN

*Cambridge*: Cambridge Intercollegiate Application Office, Kellet Lodge, Tennis Court Road, Cambridge CB2 1QJ

*Durham*: The University of Durham, Old Shire Hall, Durham DH1 3HP

*East Anglia*: The University of East Anglia, Norwich NR4 7TJ

*Edinburgh*: The University, Edinburgh EH8 9YL

*Hull*: The University of Hull, Hull North, Humberside HU6 7RX

*Kent at Canterbury*: The University Canterbury, Kent CT2 7NZ

*London*: Goldsmiths' College, Lewisham Way, London SE14 6NW
London School of Economics, Houghton Street, Aldwych WC2A 2AE
School of Oriental and African Studies, Malet Street, London WC1E 7HP
University College, Gower Street, London WC1E 6BT

*Manchester*: The University of Manchester M13 9PL

*Oxford*: Oxford College Admissions Office, University Office, Wellington Square, Oxford OX1 2JD

*St Andrews*: The University of St Andrews, College Gate, St Andrews KY16 9AJ

*Salford*: The University of Salford, Salford M5 4WT

*Stirling*: The University, Stirling FK9 4LA

*Sussex*: The University of Sussex, Sussex House, Falmer, Brighton BN1 9RH

*Swansea*: The University College of Swansea, Singleton Park, Swansea SA2 8PP

*Ulster*: The University of Ulster, Coleraine, County Londonderry BT52 1SA

Index

# Index